Encyclopedia of

DAHLIAS

Encyclopedia of

DAHLIAS

BILL McCLAREN

TIMBER PRESS
Portland ~ Cambridge

Frontispiece photo credits: Bill and S. McClaren.

Published in 2004 by

Timber Press, Inc.
The Haseltine Building
133 S.W. Second Avenue, Suite 450
Portland, Oregon 97204-3527, U.S.A.

Timber Press
2 Station Road
Swavesey
Cambridge CB4 5QJ, U.K.

www.timberpress.com

Printed in China

Library of Congress Cataloging-in-Publication Data

McClaren, Bill, 1928-
  Encyclopedia of dahlias / Bill McClaren.
    p. cm.
  Includes bibliographical references (p.   ).
  ISBN 0-88192-658-2 (hardcover)
  1. Dahlias. I. Title.
SB413.D13M39 2004
635.9'3399--dc22   2003027613

A Catalogue record for this book is also available from the British Library.

CONTENTS

FOREWORD

WHEN DAHLIA GROWERS speak about their favorite flower, they often emphasize the great diversity of forms, colors, and sizes that are available for planting in the garden. But the literature has not pictured the many cultivars that are available to growers in the United States and Canada. The most popular reference books about dahlias are written by experts in other parts of the dahlia world, and they present the most popular cultivars in England, New Zealand, Australia, France, and India—many of which are either not available or are difficult to grow successfully in many of our climates.

North American growers are left to pictures in commercial catalogs, the American Dahlia Society's slide collections, and the burgeoning resources of the Internet. The most recent "domestic" volume about dahlias on my bookshelf is the 1954 edition of *Dahlias* by Marian C. Walker (M. Barrows & Co., New York). Typical of gardening texts of the era, it includes only a limited number of color illustrations, and, of those pictured, only the redoubtable dark-foliaged peony, 'Bishop of Llandaff', is generally available.

At long last we have a dahlia book by an expert American grower that is chock-full of pictures of our favorite dahlias. For the committed dahlia grower, *Encyclopedia of Dahlias* is an invaluable reference text to check particular dahlia cultivars and their characteristics. For the general gardener with a new interest in dahlias, Bill McClaren's book is a practical guide to successfully growing dahlia plants and keeping dahlia tubers from season to season. The text is plainly written and avoids the mumbo jumbo that often accompanies expert advice. The practical suggestions are complemented with informative illustrations. The many photos of dahlia blooms identify particular cultivars that would be perfect fits for anchoring the late summer flowerbed.

For many years, short bedding dahlias have been a garden-center staple because they are hardy and have a long season of bloom. In the last two decades the tall 3 to 5 ft. (0.9 to 1.5 m) hybrid cultivars have come into their own, right along with the renaissance of interest in flower gardening. Drive down any suburban street, and you will see plants and bushes of every kind filling areas that were once closely mown green lawns. Gardening magazines frequently feature dahlias because of their striking forms and bright colors. Cable TV has introduced the home-and-garden programming genre, accessible 24 hours a day; dahlias regularly appear in garden segments and as part of indoor arrangements. With this stunning new interest in dahlias, what is really needed is a basic illustrated text for the North American audience, filled with advice and photographs of cultivars that grow well and are commercially available.

For many years Bill and Lois McClaren have been the "Johnny Appleseeds" of the American dahlia. They have encouraged dahlia growers throughout Montana and Idaho to grow dahlias, form local societies, and stage dahlia shows. They have been leaders in the American Dahlia Society. As proprietors of Alpen Gardens for many years, they encouraged hybridizers and made new cultivars available to dahlia enthusiasts. Through their extended experience with the dahlia, they have gained a wealth of knowledge and useful information. *Encyclopedia of Dahlias* is the culmination of a lifelong love affair; it deserves a place on the bookshelf of every dahlia grower and will also double as a great gift to spread the word about this most beautiful, diverse, and easy-to-grow garden flower.

HARRY A. RISSETTO
Trustee, American Dahlia Society
Contributing Editor, *Bulletin of the American Dahlia Society*

7

PREFACE

I found great satisfaction in exchanging and sharing information with students throughout my teaching career; as a garden hobbyist, I was asked to teach a class in beginning gardening in which I was able to explore many areas of gardening. Paul Hovey, a local Montana dahlia grower, introduced me to the world of dahlias. Soon after I started growing dahlias Paul passed away, and with him I lost a very close friend and my source of dahlia information. Our nearest dahlia society was in Spokane, Washington, a distance of 240 mi. (400 km), which made it difficult to receive timely dahlia information. Local gardeners often told me that dahlias could not be grown successfully in Montana, with our short growing season, but by using good growing methods and early dahlia varieties I found it was possible.

The information I read in garden magazines and dahlia literature often presented inconsistencies in the growing and propagation of dahlias, spurring me to research current practices and try new approaches to growing dahlias. My enthusiasm for growing dahlias attracted other gardeners to the dahlia world, resulting in the establishment of the first dahlia society in Montana in 1989.

Growing dahlias for the past 40 years has been a great educational experience. I spent 30 of these years as a hybridizer and 20 as a commercial grower. I have been able to share information on growing dahlias with gardeners, members of our dahlia society, dahlia growers throughout the world, and hundreds of students in dahlia judging schools. The greatest change I have made during my growing experience has been to grow dahlias organically.

The experience of writing *Encyclopedia of Dahlias* has been exciting and rewarding. With many countries of the world growing thousands of dahlia varieties, it was a challenge to know where to begin. Since it is an impossible task to cover all the different climates and weather conditions throughout the world, I have attempted to give basic information on growing dahlias which can be adopted by all growers. Information on growing dahlias organically is limited; this book was an opportunity to share what knowledge I have gained from other growers and the literature with others. The dahlia is changing rapidly each year; many hybridizers are introducing new forms, sizes, and colors, making the dahlia the flower of the future.

This encyclopedia features more than 800 photos; in chapters 2 through 7, descriptions of individual varieties arranged by size, form, and color give the readers an overview of the dahlia. Each photo's caption includes the ADS (American Dahlia Society) class number and the name of the dahlia, in single quotes; its size, form, color, hybridizer, year of introduction (an asterisk [*] indicates the exact date of introduction is not known), and country of origin, in parentheses; notes on the flower and any awards it has received; and credit to the photographer or the image's provenance. Individual chapters tell how to grow dahlias and how to care for tubers; these chapters are meant to be a manual for all interested gardeners and dahlia growers as they continue to expand their knowledge of the dahlia.

The hybridizer who names the dahlias does not always use "traditional" spellings; however, once approved by the ADS, the name remains as presented. I made a diligent effort to determine each cultivar's correct name, hybridizer, year of introduction, and country of origin; I have grown, judged, or observed a majority of the dahlias presented in the book, and for any errors, I ask your understanding.

I wrote this encyclopedia for new and experienced gardeners who would like to grow dahlias. I want to share information that will be helpful to the dahlia enthusiasts who grow both for fun and for profit.

ACKNOWLEDGMENTS

Writing this book was one of the most enjoyable and satisfying projects I have accomplished in my lifetime. A special thanks to my wife and family, who furnished suggestions and encouragement and worked diligently typing and proofing the book.

Thanks to the Montana Dahlia Society and the Pacific Southwest Dahlia Conference, for giving permission to photograph their shows, and to dahlia growers Ray and Iris Jones, John Kestell, Ken and Marilyn Masurat, and Mike Valler, for letting photographers tramp through their gardens. Thanks to those who furnished slides for the book: American Dahlia Society Slide Library, LaVerne Bartel, Slide Library Chair; Dick Ambrose, Washington State, USA; Ben Bartel, Wisconsin, USA; Stephen L. Boley, Washington State, USA; Alan Fisher, Maryland, USA; Ginny Hunt, California, USA; Walter Jack, New Zealand; Yusaku Konishi, Japan; Martin Kral, Washington State, USA; Jim Rowse, Washington State, USA; Wayne Shantz, Oregon, USA; and Swan Island Dahlias, Oregon, USA. A special thanks to Dayle Saar for her valuable research and the information she furnished on the species dahlias.

I am greatly indebted to the American Dahlia Society, the Officers, and Executive Board for permission to use their many years of records and information on the dahlia. Without their input, this book would never have been written.

CHAPTER 1

The Dahlia

WHY GROW DAHLIAS? The answers are as varied as the dahlia itself. Because dahlia hybrids offer such diversity in size, form, and color, every grower will likely discover his or her own individual reason for growing dahlias. Home gardeners enjoy growing and sharing dahlias with their friends and neighbors. Dahlia hobbyists are involved in the finer points of dahlia cultivation and often compete in shows with the hope of displaying a grand-champion flower. Dahlia hybridizers specialize in the creation of new and different forms of dahlias. Commercial growers sell tubers, plants, and cut flowers to customers and florists.

THE PLANT

The dahlia is a member of the Asteraceae, or composite family, and is usually propagated from a tuber. In frost-free areas it can be raised as a perennial. The tubers cannot tolerate frost so must be grown as annuals in areas where the ground freezes. Dahlias thrive in all types of soil and in every country in the world. The size of the tuber does not determine the size of the plant or flower. Dahlias prefer full sun to partial shade.

The size, form, and color determine the variety of the flower. Daylength has an effect on the formation of the bud: dahlias need long days for good bud development. The flowers usually appear six to eight weeks after the tuber is planted, depending on the variety. Varieties with the largest blooms need additional time to produce their first flowers. Flowers will be more numerous as the season progresses and will continue

Each stem contains the main center bud, a growth bud (l), and a small bud (r). Photo by McClaren.

Dahlia leaves showing three leaflets and five leaflets. Photo by McClaren.

blooming until frost or when the plant goes into dormancy. The dahlia is among the longest-flowering plants, making it a perfect choice for potted plants, cut flowers, and landscapes. Tubers develop and multiply during the growing period and are retained for stock the following year.

Over the last two centuries the dahlia has been hybridized from a small number of species to one of the largest arrays of forms, colors, and sizes of any flower grown. The height of the plants ranges from 6 in. (15 cm) to 20 ft. (6 m), depending on the variety. The height of each variety is determined by environmental conditions such as soil, fertilizers, water, and climate. The size of the tuber also varies with the variety and, again, has no relationship to plant or bloom size. In the last 100 years nearly 50,000 named dahlia varieties have been developed, listed, and registered in over 570 classes. The hybridizer names each new introduction. The Royal Horticultural Society is responsible for the internationally accepted nomenclature for naming dahlias. The American Dahlia Society (ADS) compiles a composite list of dahlias in American shows, many of which have been hybridized throughout the world. More hybridizers are active than at any time in history, and the rapid addition of new forms, sizes, and colors makes the dahlia an exciting flower to grow.

The dahlia plant is composed of two parts: growth below ground and growth above ground. The underground growth is the roots and tubers, above ground, the stalk, stem, branches, and foliage. In horticultural and botanical texts the terms stalk and stem are used interchangeably; for clarity's sake, the ADS defines the stalk as the main plant growth with nodes and leaves, and the terminal or top growth of the stalk, above the highest set of leaves, is called the stem. Nodes grow from the junction of the leaf and main stalk and develop to form new branches. Each stem and branch contains the main center bud, a growth branch with a bud, and a small side bud. The plant has opposite and decussate leaves with three to five leaflets. Some plants have more than one set of leaves at a single node. The foliage color ranges from light green to dark mahogany.

The flower is composite, composed of ray florets, disc flowers, and bracts. The disc or center flowers bear the pistil (stigma, style, and ovary) and the stamen (filament and anther, or pollen sac). There are two different flower formations: open-centered flowers are those with the disc showing, surrounded by one or more rows of ray florets; close-centered flowers have multiple rows of ray florets entirely covering the disc and curving back to the stem. There are 7 open-centered forms and 11 close-centered forms.

Dahlia foliage in a range of colors. Photo by McClaren.

The bracts with the ray florets removed and surrounding the disc flowers. Photo by McClaren.

The composite flower is made up of the ray florets (outside), disc flowers (center), and greenish bracts, which are often hidden by the ray florets. Photo by McClaren.

Disc flowers and ray florets. Photo by McClaren.

An open-centered flower with disc showing and surrounded by ray florets. Photo by McClaren.

Disc flowers showing pistils and stamens, which contain the pollen-bearing anther. Photo by McClaren.

A close-centered flower: multiple rows of ray florets entirely covering the disc. Photo by McClaren.

USES OF DAHLIAS

With so many forms, sizes, and colors, dahlias have many uses. Originally, florists used them nearly exclusively for baskets and bouquets, especially when a large display of color was desired. Florists now use dahlias for all forms of arrangements and artistic designs. Dahlias are principally grown in flowerbeds. They can also be used as a container plant on decks and patios, and the small varieties are grown successfully in window boxes. Dahlias dry well for attractive, long-lasting floral displays. The earthen colors acquired from dahlia flowers are used for dyeing natural yarns and fabrics. Landscapers and nurserymen find the dahlia a useful addition to their designs and trade.

Gardeners throughout the world have discovered the immense satisfaction and pleasure of growing dahlias. Through hybridization, exciting new varieties continue to be introduced. The possible uses for the dahlia are limited only by the grower's imagination.

A basket of dahlias. Photo by McClaren.

An artistic arrangement using dahlias. Photo by McClaren.

A bouquet incorporating dahlias. Photo by McClaren.

The dahlia as a potted plant. Photo by McClaren.

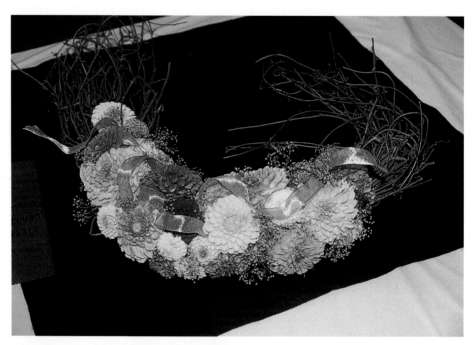

Arrangement of dried dahlias. Photo by Alan Fisher.

Dahlias in the landscape. Photo by Walter Jack.

CHAPTER 2

AA and A Size

The American Dahlia Society classifies dahlias over 10 in. (25 cm) as AA size and those from 8 to 10 in. (20 to 25 cm) as A size. Prior to 1975, the ADS classified all dahlia flowers over 8 in. (20 cm) as A size; however, hybridizers developed dahlias larger than 10 in. (25 cm) in such numbers that the creation of a new size classification was justified.

These spectacular large blooms provide a captivating display of color, making these dahlias longtime favorites of dahlia growers. Before the present classification, large dahlias were commonly called dinner plates; since dahlias are now classified by size, it is preferable to use the more accurate AA and A designations.

The photos in this chapter represent the 15 color classes and include examples of the formal decorative, informal decorative, semi-cactus, straight cactus, incurved cactus, and laciniated forms.

AA PHOTOS

002 'Kelvin Floodlight' (AA FD Y, McDougall, 1959, Australia) is clear bright yellow. It grows in all areas on a healthy plant, mid blooming, with strong straight stems. Wins its Class, Best AA Formal Decorative in Show, Best Bloom in Show, Largest Bloom in Show, Cream of the Crop, and Fabulous Fifty. Global Publishing

006 'Masurao' (AA FD R, Konishi, 1994*, Japan) first appeared in the midwestern United States and has been a consistent winner at ADS shows. Tolerates heat and grows throughout the United States and Canada. Wins its Class and Cream of the Crop. Ben Bartel

014 'Jeremy Boldt' (AA FD V L/W, Cunningham, 1999, USA) has been winning in the western United States with its color and form; greater distribution will increase its popularity in other areas of the world. Wins Cream of the Crop. S. McClaren

021 'Mingus Whitney' (AA ID W, Mingus, 1997, USA) has grown in popularity each year, with the greatest number of wins in the western United States and Canada, and in areas with cool weather and humidity. Wins in a very competitive Class, Best AA in Show, and Cream of the Crop. S. McClaren

021 'Penhill Cream Giant' (AA ID W, Maritz, 1997, South Africa) will enjoy increasing popularity as distribution to North American growers improves. Wins in a difficult Class. S. McClaren

021 'Walter Hardisty' (AA ID W, Gentile, 1975, USA). Lynn B. Dudley and Stanley Johnson awards. This clear white dahlia has perfectly formed petals and full petalage, giving it great depth. Does exceptionally well in midwestern and eastern United States and Canada. The tubers tend to be difficult to keep in long storage. Wins its Class, Best AA in Show, Best Bloom in Show, Cream of the Crop, and Fabulous Fifty. Hard to beat. Ben Bartel

022 'Ivory Palaces' (AA ID Y, Simon, 1992*, USA), an enormous dahlia, grows in popularity each year. Easy to grow on a healthy 5 ft. (1.5 m) plant with good tuber production. Wins its Class, Best AA in Show, Cream of the Crop, and Fabulous Fifty. Popular in all areas of Canada and the United States. Alan Fisher

023 'Rowse Seedling' (AA ID OR, Rowse, USA) is a great new seedling with the full petalage and attractive color its class needs. An easy-to-grow dahlia that growers of AA flowers will want to add to their collections. Jim Rowse

024 'Croydon Serene' (AA ID PK, Brand, 1966, Australia) is blends of light lavender-pink in the margins with a darker center. It is an easy plant to grow, with many long-keeping tubers, and a successful seed parent of many flowers, including 'Edna C'. Wins its Class, Best Informal Decorative in Show, and Cream of the Crop. Ben Bartel

023 'Orange Flame' (AA ID OR, Comstock, 1982, USA) is orange blends with petals of many forms: some have laciniated splits, others are incurved cactus, others informal decorative. The bloom is often too large for the stem to support, making the flower side facing. An attractive garden flower. ADS slide library

023 'Sam Huston' (AA ID OR, Huston, 1994, Canada) is a very popular AA flower introduced by Earl Huston, an outstanding hybridizer of large dahlias. It grows on a strong 5 ft. (1.5 m) well-branched plant with many early blooms and is easy to grow with healthy tubers that keep for long periods in storage. Wins its Class, Best AA in Show, Cream of the Crop, and Fabulous Fifty. McClaren

025 'Belle of Barmera' (AA ID DP, Simon, 1987, USA) is an outstanding dark pink with good depth and full petalage. Easy to grow on a tall healthy plant. Wins its Class, Largest Dahlia in Show, and Cream of the Crop. S. McClaren

026 'Bodacious' (AA ID R, Swan Island Dahlias, 2002, USA). Derrill W. Hart Award. This bright orange-red with a yellow reverse is a ball of fire. Ideal petals and full petalage make it a great show flower. It produces excellent blooms in all areas of the United States and Canada. Wins its Class, Best AA in Show, Best Informal Decorative in Show, and Cream of the Crop. Swan Island Dahlias

027 'Envy' (AA ID DR, Castro, 1965, USA) is nonfading dark red with well-formed petals. Easy to grow with strong straight stems. Wins in a very competitive Class, Best AA Informal Decorative in Show, Best AA in Show, and Cream of the Crop. Ben Bartel

027 'Zorro' (AA ID DR, Geisert, 1987, USA). Lynn B. Dudley, Derrill W. Hart, and Stanley Johnson awards. Madlyn Geisert introduced many excellent flowers, but 'Zorro', her most outstanding, should be the number-one choice for anyone who likes to grow enormous flowers. It grows on tall 6 ft. (1.8 m) well-branched plants with early blooms. Easy to grow and an attractive show and garden dahlia. Wins Best Informal Decorative in Show, Best AA in Show, Largest in Show, Best Bloom in Show, Cream of the Crop, and Fabulous Fifty. McClaren

028 'Bella S' (AA ID L, Strunz, 1995, USA), a light lavender of great size, grows on a tall healthy fully branched plant, tolerates heat, and is easy to grow. Wins its Class, Best AA in Show, Largest in Show, Cream of the Crop, and Fabulous Fifty. McClaren

028 'Lavender Ruffles' (AA ID L, Swan Island Dahlias, 2000, USA), a sport of 'Purple Taiheijo', has large, wide, ruffled, pastel lavender petals. It grows on a low to medium plant and blooms into late fall. Swan Island Dahlias

030 'Shiloh Noelle' (AA ID LB W/L, Cunningham, 1986, USA), a pleasing blend with excellent form, has always been in a very competitive Class. Makes an attractive display as a grouping. S. McClaren

030 'Sir Alf Ramsey' (AA ID LB L/W, Cleaver, 1999, UK) is showing well as a new arrival in the United States and Canada. Easy to grow and early to flower, with many lavender and white blooms and good tuber production. Wins its Class, Best AA in Show, Cream of the Crop, and Fabulous Fifty. ADS slide library

031 'Ben Huston' (AA ID BR, Huston, 1992, Canada) is clear orange-bronze with full petalage. Extra-large early blooms are carried on a strong healthy 6 ft. (1.8 m) fully branched plant. Easy to grow. Wins its Class, Largest Dahlia in Show, and Cream of the Crop. S. McClaren

031 'Croydon Masterpiece' (AA ID BR, Brand, 1948*, Australia) is a blend of yellow-orange in the margins blending to a bronzey orange in the center. The pleated petals are pointed; some are formal decorative. Wins in a very competitive Class and Largest Bloom in Show. McClaren

041 'Kenora Clyde' (AA SC W, Leroux, 1988, USA). Lynn B. Dudley Award. This is among the tallest dahlia plants in the garden, growing to 7 ft. (2.1 m) and fully branched; it blooms prolifically mid to late season but is well worth the wait— an excellent bloom for late shows. Tolerates heat. Wins its Class, Best AA in Show, Largest Bloom in Show, Best Bloom in Show, Cream of the Crop, and Fabulous Fifty. Since being introduced it has never relinquished these honors. McClaren

042 'Inland Dynasty' (AA SC Y, Anselmo, 1992, USA). Derrill W. Hart and Stanley Johnson awards. An instant success, winning Cream of the Crop and Fabulous Fifty in 1993 and the Stanley Johnson award in 1994, the only dahlia ever to have won the award in its second year after being introduced. An excellent tuber producer, it can be grown throughout the world and blooms early with many show flowers. Wins Best Semi-Cactus in Show, Best AA Dahlia in Show, Best Bloom in Show, and Largest Bloom in Show. McClaren

043 'Alfred C' (AA SC OR, Almand, 1974, USA). Derrill W. Hart Award. This tall healthy 5 ft. (1.5 m) dahlia boasts many early blooms and is easy to grow with good tuber production. Among its several sports is 'Alpen Bob', a variegated flower. Wins its Class, Best AA in Show, Best Semi-Cactus in Show, Cream of the Crop, and Fabulous Fifty. McClaren

043 'Conquistador' (AA SC OR, Traff, 1974, USA), a dark orange, is among the largest dahlias hybridized in the United States. It is not an easy dahlia to grow and propagate, and it is difficult to find stock. Wins its Class, Largest Dahlia in Show, and Cream of the Crop.
Dick Ambrose

046 'Danum Meteor' (AA SC R, Oscroft Nursery, 1996, UK) is clear bright non-fading red with full petalage. It grows on a healthy plant with stout straight stems. Wins in a competitive Class, Best AA Semi-Cactus in Show, and Cream of the Crop. Ben Bartel

047 'Dr. Les' (AA SC DR, Almand, 1975, USA). Derrill W. Hart Award. This non-fading clean dark red with full petalage is easy to grow on a tall healthy plant with great stems. It produces many tubers that keep well in storage. Wins in a very competitive Class, Best AA Semi-Cactus in Show, Best AA Bloom in Show, and Cream of the Crop. Ben Bartel

046 'Creve Coeur' (AA SC R, Simon, 1992*, USA). Derrill W. Hart Award. Originally classified as an informal decorative, this dahlia was reclassified as a semi-cactus in 1996. Wins in both classes, Best AA in Show, Largest Bloom in Show, Cream of the Crop, and Fabulous Fifty. Its enormous red flower, one of the largest blooms in the garden, is borne on a tall healthy plant with many early blooms. McClaren

046 'Wildman' (AA SC R, Traff, 1984, USA) is a great red with lighter tips that make the bloom sparkle. Excellent form with full petalage and easy to grow. It is a healthy fully branched plant with early blooms, does well in all climates, and tolerates heat. Wins its Class, Best AA Semi-Cactus, Best AA in Show, Cream of the Crop, and Fabulous Fifty. McClaren

047 'Gregory Stephen' (AA SC DR, Swan Island Dahlias, 1997, USA), a giant true red with yellow reverse on the tips, has some twisted petals and full petalage. It grows on a healthy plant and blooms from mid to late season.
Swan Island Dahlias

050 'Gargantuan' (AA SC LB PK/Y, L. Connell, 1994, USA) is a blend of pastel shades of pink and yellow with excellent form and continuous blooms throughout the season. It grows on a healthy 5 ft. (1.5 m) plant, is easy to grow, and tolerates heat. Wins in a difficult Class. Alan Fisher

050 'LeVonne Splinter' (AA SC LB Y/OR, Comstock, 1978, USA). Derrill W. Hart and Lynn B. Dudley awards. This is a bright yellow dahlia blending to a clean orange in the margins, well formed and with full petalage. It is easy to grow on a tall healthy plant with strong straight stems. Does best on the west coast of Canada and the United States. Wins in a competitive Class, Best AA Semi-Cactus in Show, Best AA in Show, Best Bloom in Show, Cream of the Crop, and Fabulous Fifty. Alan Fisher

050 'Mom and Dad' (AA SC LB Y/PK, Metzger, 1993, USA) was reclassified in 2003 from informal decorative to semi-cactus and wins in either class. It is an attractive color combination, easy to grow and show. Huge blooms are carried on a tall healthy plant. Tolerates heat. Wins in a very competitive Class and Cream of the Crop. Ben Bartel

050 'Nasu-No-Hikari' (AA SC LB OR/Y, Konishi, 2001, Japan), a pastel yellow center blending to a soft orange, has excellent consistent form with full petalage. It is easy to grow on a strong healthy plant, well branched and with many blooms held on strong straight stems. Wins in a very competitive Class. Yusaku Konishi

051 'Irene's Pride' (AA SC BR, Szalkowski, 1990, USA). Lynn B. Dudley Award. This is a dahlia to be grown by all large-flower enthusiasts. Grows on a healthy tall plant with many show blooms. Ideal in the late season. Wins its Class, Best AA in Show, Best Bloom in Show, Cream of the Crop, and Fabulous Fifty. Ben Bartel

052 'Mr. Larry' (AA SC FL, Comstock, 1975, USA) is among the oldest AA flowers still winning its Class and Cream of the Crop. Many blooms are borne on a strong healthy well-branched plant. Easy to grow, and a prolific tuber producer. Tolerates heat. S. McClaren

061 'Hy Mom' (AA IC W, W. Holland, 2001, Canada) is without blemishes or blushes, a perfect form with full petalage recurving to the stem. It is easy to grow with many huge early blooms carried on a strong tall healthy plant, fully branched. An outstanding show flower, it will be a favorite AA flower for many years. Wins its Class and Cream of the Crop. S. McClaren

070 'Hana Hitosuji' (AA C LB PK/Y, Konishi, 1998*, Japan), one of Konishi's most popular flowers in the United States, is a pleasing blend of pink and yellow. It grows on a strong healthy plant, early to flower with many show blooms. Wins its Class and Cream of the Crop. S. McClaren

A PHOTOS

061 'Spike' (AA C W, Frasier, 1967, USA), introduced as an A but since reclassified, is one of the very few AA white cacti. Pure white blooms are borne on a healthy plant that produces strong tubers. Wins its Class. McClaren

101 'Gemma Darling' (A FD W, Dilley, 1993, UK) is ivory-white with pleated petals, inconsistent form, and full petalage. Originally classified as an AA but changed to A in 2003. It is easy to grow on a healthy plant. Wins its Class, Best A Formal Decorative. McClaren

101 'White Alvas' (A FD W, Mills, 1978, UK), a clean white with perfect petal form and full petalage, is a sport of 'Alva's Supreme' with all the same characteristics. It is easy to grow on a healthy plant with strong straight stems and produces good tubers that keep well in storage. Wins in a competitive Class, Best A Formal Decorative, and Cream of the Crop. ADS slide library

107 'Drummer Boy' (A FD DR, Baynes, 1960, Australia), an outstanding nonfading dark red with excellent petal form and full petalage, could easily be grown for the next half century. It has healthy plant growth, strong healthy tuber production, and early blooms. Wins its Class and Cream of the Crop. McClaren

108 'Clint's Climax' (A FD L, Beard, 1987, South Africa) is blends of lavender with petals that split in hot weather. Does well in all areas but produces the best blooms with some shade. Wins its Class, Best A Formal Decorative, and Cream of the Crop. McClaren

108 'Elma Elizabeth' (A FD L, Redd, 1993, USA), a clean clear lavender with ideal petal form and full petalage, first won as an informal decorative and continued winning after being reclassified in 1996: great substance and strong stems make it an excellent cut and show flower. Many mid to late blooms are carried on a very strong tall healthy fully branched plant. Excellent tuber production; grows in all areas and tolerates heat. Wins its Class, Best A in Show, Best Bloom in Show, Cream of the Crop, and Fabulous Fifty. Ben Bartel

108 'Polyand' (A FD L, Young, 1953, Australia) is an early Australian dahlia with attractively pleated, clean lavender petals. It grows on a strong healthy plant with strong straight stems. The tubers keep well in storage. Wins its Class, Cream of the Crop, and Fabulous Fifty. Dick Ambrose

110 'Almand Joy' (A FD LB W/L, Almand, 1968, USA). Derrill W. Hart Award. This sport of 'Kidd's Climax' is a pleasing blend that is easy to grow on a strong healthy 4 ft. (1.2 m) plant. Good tuber production and a successful seed parent. Wins its difficult Class, Best A Formal Decorative in Show, Best A in Show, and Best Bloom in Show. McClaren

110 'Kidd's Climax' (A FD LB Y/PK, Kidd, 1940, New Zealand) is the most grown and shown dahlia worldwide. The plant is healthy, and the perfect blooms are ideal for the show table. If it has a weakness it is in the tubers, which tend to disintegrate during long storage; propagate from cuttings or pot tubers. Easy to grow, tolerates heat. Wins its Class, Best A Bloom in Show, Best Bloom in Show, Cream of the Crop, and Fabulous Fifty. S. McClaren

110 'Mabel Ann' (A FD LB OR/Y, Adley, 1995, UK) is a light blend of pastel orange and yellow. Wins its difficult class in the eastern United States and Canada. Alan Fisher

115 'Mrs. McDonald Quill' (A FD BI DR/W, Douglas, 1955, New Zealand), a dark red with evenly spaced white tips, has pointed twisted petals when first developing. It is among the largest bicolors, and, as with many, it tends to burn on the tips in hot full sun; shading improves this weakness. Badly needed and wins its Class. Ben Bartel

121 'Maisie Mooney' (A ID W, Mooney, 1994, Canada) is a clean, sparkling white whose form and size will depend on where it is grown and how it is cared for while developing. Originally an AA informal decorative (and still often seen thus in shows), it was changed to an A formal decorative in 1996 and to an A informal decorative in 1998. Easy to grow with perfect petal formation, full petalage, and excellent tuber production, it is a flower for all growers of large blooms. Wins its Class, Best AA in Show, Best A in Show, Best Bloom in Show, Cream of the Crop, and Fabulous Fifty. Jim Rowse

121 'Snowbound' (A ID W, Swan Island Dahlias, 1997, USA). Derrill W. Hart Award. This clear white with well-formed petals and full petalage grows in all climates on a healthy fully branched plant with many early blooms. Easy to grow and produces many tubers that keep well in storage. Wins its Class, Best A Informal Decorative in Show, Best A in Show, and Cream of the Crop. Swan Island Dahlias

122 'Cynthia Louise' (A ID Y, Swan Island Dahlias, 1991, USA), a sport of 'Kidd's Climax', is a soft pastel yellow with full petalage. It was reclassified in 1999 from a formal decorative to an informal decorative, both difficult classes. Wins its Class and Best Informal Decorative in Show. McClaren

123 'Cherokee Gold' (A ID OR, Ricks, 1982, USA) is bright orange with full petalage recurving to the stem; the majority of the petals are informal decorative, some are semi-cactus. It is easy to grow on a tall healthy plant that prefers shade. Grows and shows well in midwestern Canada and the United States. Wins its Class and Cream of the Crop. McClaren

124 'Elsie Huston' (A ID PK, Huston, 1989*, Canada) is a blend of lavender-pink with full petalage. Prefers some shade for the brightest color. It is easy to grow in all areas on a tall healthy plant with many blooms and excellent tuber production. Wins its Class, Best A in Show, Cream of the Crop, and Fabulous Fifty. McClaren

125 'Hamari Girl' (A ID DP, Ensum, 1960, UK), an early dahlia from the United Kingdom and a favorite of many, has excellent petal form and a clear dark pink color. When first grown in the United States it was classified as an A formal decorative, changed in 1975 to an AA formal decorative, reclassified as an AA informal decorative in 1984, and changed to an A informal decorative in 1988: the majority of the petals are informal decorative with scattered formal decorative petals. Easy to grow on a healthy plant. Wins its Class, Cream of the Crop, and Fabulous Fifty. Dick Ambrose

125 'Islander' (A ID DP, Wickey, 1983, USA) is blends of light and darker pink with twisted petals recurving to the stem. Many late blooms are borne on a tall healthy plant on tall straight stems. Produces an abundance of healthy tubers that keep well in storage. Wins its Class, Best A Informal Decorative in Show, Best A in Show, Best Bloom in Show, Cream of the Crop, and Fabulous Fifty. Ben Bartel

127 'Spartacus' (A ID DR, M. Senior, 1993, USA). Lynn B. Dudley, Derrill W. Hart, and Stanley Johnson awards. A flower that all hybridizers dream of finding in the seedling garden, 'Spartacus' has been a consistent winner since its introduction. In 1997 it was reclassified as a formal decorative but changed back to an informal decorative in 1999. It is a perfect dahlia in the garden: well branched, does not fade, easy to grow, and tolerates heat, and its excellent substance and strong stems make it a great show and cut flower. Excellent tuber production and easy to get on the show bench. Wins its Class, Best A Informal Decorative in Show. Best A in Show, Best Bloom in Show, Cream of the Crop, and Fabulous Fifty. Ben Bartel

128 'Kohan-No-Yado' (A ID L, Konishi, 1993*, Japan) offers shades of lavender with excellent petal form and full petalage recurving to the stem. It is easy to grow on a healthy fully branched plant with many blooms. Wins its Class. Yusaku Konishi

128 'Oregon Reign' (A ID L, Swan Island Dahlias, 2000, USA) is a blend of lavender with darker lavender outlines on each petal and full petalage. Easy to grow on a tall healthy plant and an attractive garden flower. Swan Island Dahlias

130 'Gitt's Perfection' (A ID LB L/W, Swan Island Dahlias, 1997, USA) is a light blend of lavender blending to white in the center of the bloom with good petal form. It blooms late in the season on a 3.5 ft. (1.05 m) plant and produces tubers that keep well in storage. Tolerates heat. Wins its large competitive Class, Cream of the Crop, and Fabulous Fifty. McClaren

128 'Lavengro' (A ID L, Barnes, 1953, UK) is a clean lavender with full petalage. It is easy to grow on strong straight stems. Wins its Class and Cream of the Crop. Dick Ambrose

130 'Ferncliff Illusion' (A ID LB W/L, D. Jack, 1994, Canada) is a blend of white with lavender tips and a consistent form. Wins in a competitive Class. McClaren

130 'Mingus Nicole' (A ID LB PK/Y, Mingus, 2000, USA). Derrill W. Hart Award. This yellow blending to pink offers perfect petal form and full petalage recurving to the stem. It grows in all climates on a healthy plant with many blooms on strong straight stems. Wins Best Single and Triple A Informal Decorative in Show, Best Bloom in Show, and Cream of the Crop. Wayne Shantz

130 'Mingus Wesley' (A ID LB L/W, Mingus, 1997, USA) is white blending to lavender at the tips. It grows on a strong healthy plant with good tuber production and full petalage. Wins in a very competitive Class and Cream of the Crop. McClaren

131 'Hamari Gold' (A ID BR, Ensum, 1984, UK) is a sharp bronze with excellent form and full petalage. It grows on a healthy plant and prefers cool weather and humidity. Wins its Class, Best A Informal Decorative in Show, Cream of the Crop, and Fabulous Fifty. S. McClaren

133 'Swan's Sunset' (A ID DB R/OR, Swan Island Dahlias, 1990, USA) is a red-orange with full petalage blending to canary-yellow tips. It has some semi-cactus petals and could be considered a bicolor. Easy to grow on a healthy plant with blooms of good substance on strong straight stems, making it a good cut and show flower. Wins its Class and Best A Informal Decorative in Show. Swan Island Dahlias

130 'Swan's Desert Storm' (A ID LB Y/PK, Swan Island Dahlias, 1992, USA) is soft golden yellow blending to pink. It grows on a mid-sized plant with many blooms. Wins in a very competitive Class. Swan Island Dahlias

132 'Dyn-O-Mite' (A ID FL, Swan Island Dahlias, 2003, USA) is red-orange with full petalage and a yellow reverse that makes the center flame. Easy to grow, it blooms mid to late season on a healthy plant, just in time for late shows and fall arrangements. Swan Island Dahlias

134 'Alpen Bob' (A ID V L/PR, McClaren, 1999, USA). Derrill W. Hart Award. A sport of 'Alfred C' with many of the same fine qualities, 'Alpen Bob' grows on a tall healthy plant with good tuber production and consistent, even variegation. Successful seed parent. Wins its Class and Best Variegated in Show. McClaren

134 'Bristol Stripe' (A ID V W/L/PR, Dearborn, 1978, USA), a vibrant variegated, is easy to grow on a healthy plant with full branching. Wins its Class and Cream of the Crop. McClaren

142 'G W's Julie B' (A SC Y, Wolfe, 2002, USA) is soft pale yellow with great full petalage and perfect petal form. It can be grown to AA size with good growing techniques. Wins in a strong Class, Best A Semi-Cactus in Show, and Cream of the Crop. S. McClaren

143 'Lloyd Huston' (A SC OR, Huston, 1983, Canada) is blends of pastel orange and has pleated petals. Does well in midwestern Canada and the United States. Wins its Class, Best A Semi-Cactus in Show, Best A in Show, and Cream of the Crop. ADS slide library

141 'Kenora Jubilee' (A SC W, Leroux, 2002, USA), another outstanding dahlia hybridized by Gordon Leroux, is a strong healthy plant with perfect petal form and full petalage. Wins its Class, Best Semi-Cactus A in Show, Best Bloom in Show, Cream of the Crop, and Fabulous Fifty. Alan Fisher

142 'Janal Amy' (A SC Y, A. Jones, 1999, UK) is bright yellow with perfect petal form and full petalage recurving to the stem. Grows on a healthy plant with dark green foliage. Does best in cool weather with high humidity. Wins in a very competitive Class, Best A Semi-Cactus in Show, Best A in Show, Best Bloom in Show, Cream of the Crop, and Fabulous Fifty. Alan Fisher

143 'Snoho William' (A SC OR, Bonneywell, 1997, USA) is blends of orange with incurved, not flat, petals; petals tend to develop into different forms. It grows on a healthy plant with early blooms. Wins its Class. ADS slide library

145 'Persian Monarch' (A SC DP, Bruidegom, 1968, Holland) is very dark pink with well-formed petals and full petalage. It was introduced as an A but reclassified as an AA in 1975 and changed back to an A in 1996. Wins in a competitive Class and Cream of the Crop. Dick Ambrose

146 'Cynthia Huston' (A SC R, Huston, 1994*, Canada) is brilliant red with well-formed petals and full petalage. It is easy to grow on a tall healthy plant with many blooms. Wins in a competitive Class, Best A Semi-Cactus in Show, Best A in Show, and Cream of the Crop. McClaren

146 'Kenora Wildfire' (A SC R, Leroux, 1989, USA). Lynn B. Dudley Award. 'Kenora Wildfire' has been in the winner circle since it was introduced, originally as an informal decorative and reclassified as a semi-cactus in 2003. Wins its Class, Best Semi-Cactus in Show, Best A in Show, Best Bloom in Show, Cream of the Crop, and Fabulous Fifty in both classifications. It is easy to grow with full petalage and great color, and produces fine tubers. Does well in all areas and tolerates heat. Ben Bartel

145 'William R' (A SC DP, Redd, 1990, USA). Derrill W. Hart Award. This dahlia is blends of pink with well-formed petals and full petalage. Does best in cool weather with high humidity. Wins its Class, Best A Semi-Cactus in Show, Best A in Show, Best Bloom in Show, Cream of the Crop, and Fabulous Fifty. Ben Bartel

146 'Homer T' (A SC R, Almand, 1990, USA) is nonfading red with long pointed petals. It tends to lack full petalage, giving a sparse appearance. Wins in a very competitive Class. ADS slide library

150 'Jan Lennon' (A SC LB L/W, Sibley, 1978, Australia) is a great blend of white and lavender on strong straight stems. It prefers cool weather with high humidity. Wins in a very competitive Class, Best A Semi-Cactus in Show, Cream of the Crop, and Fabulous Fifty. Wayne Shantz

150 'Oreti Harvest' (A SC LB PK/Y, W. Jack, New Zealand) is a blend with perfectly formed well-placed petals and full petalage recurving to the stem. It is an easy plant to grow on a tall healthy plant producing many blooms with good substance. Wins its Class and when fully distributed should be a winner of higher awards. Walter Jack

150 'Skipley Grande' (A SC LB Y/DP, R. Williams, 2001, USA). Derrill W. Hart Award. This dahlia, with perfect petal form and full petalage recurving to the stem, is easy to grow on a healthy fully branched plant with many early blooms. Wins its Class, Best A in Show, Best Semi-Cactus in Show, Best Bloom in Show, and Cream of the Crop the first year after being introduced. McClaren

151 'Campos Howard M' (A SC BR, Campobello Dahlia Farms, 1999, USA) is orange-bronze with a majority of semi-cactus petals and full petalage. It grows on a healthy plant with blooms on strong stems and of firm substance, making it a valuable show and cut flower. Wins its Class. Wayne Shantz

150 'Pink Jupiter' (A SC LB PK/DP, Hardham, 1981, UK). All the Jupiter dahlias have been winners, and 'Pink Jupiter' is no exception. A great color combination with excellent form and full petalage, it grows well on the west coast of Canada and the United States, where the temperature is cooler and the humidity higher, and is also a favorite in the United Kingdom. Wins its Class, Best A Semi-Cactus in Show, Best Bloom in Show, Cream of the Crop, and Fabulous Fifty. Ben Bartel

150 'Vanquisher' (A SC LB W/L, L. Connell, 1990, USA) is white with full petalage blending to lavender on the tips. Wins in a very competitive Class. McClaren

152 'Flame' (A SC FL, Redd, 1992, USA) is bright red blending to bright yellow at the base of the petal, showing very little of the yellow. It has incurved petals and full petalage. Wins in a very competitive Class and Best A Semi-Cactus in Show. ADS slide library

153 'Daleko Jupiter' (A SC DB Y/DP, Krzywicki, 1979, UK) is clear bright yellow blending to a dark pink in the margins of the bloom. It has excellent form but tends to lack petalage. Wins its Class, Best Semi-Cactus in Show, Best Bloom in Show, and Cream of the Crop. Ben Bartel

162 'Parkland Amigo' (A IC Y, Rowse, 1999, USA) is clear bright yellow with great petal form and full petalage. It needs a cool humid environment to develop winning flowers. Wins in a difficult Class. Jim Rowse

164 'Mo Bay's Princess' (A C PK, H. and B. Brown, 1992, USA) has great form and grows well on the west coast of Canada and the United States, preferring cool weather and humidity. Wins its Class and Best A Cactus in Show. S. McClaren

161 'Hy Abalone' (A C W, W. Holland, 2002, Canada) is clean white with twisted petals. It is easy to grow on a tall healthy plant with blooms on strong straight stems—a cut and show flower. Wins in a competitive Class. McClaren

163 'Hollyhill Electra' (A IC OR, T. and M. Kennedy, 2001, USA) won its Class and Cream of the Crop the first year on the show table. It has great form, full petalage, and grows in all areas of the United States and Canada. Easy to grow on a healthy full-branched plant. S. McClaren

166 'My Guide' (A IC R, Bruidegom, 1974, Holland) is clean red with well-formed, full petalage, which many early incurved cacti lacked. Introduced as a B but changed to an A in 1987. Wins its competitive Class and Cream of the Crop. Dick Ambrose

166 'Skipley Valentine' (A C R, R. Williams, 1993, USA) is a beautiful non-fading red with excellent form. It grows on a healthy plant over 6 ft. (1.8 m) with many early blooms. Easy to grow and produces an abundance of tubers. Wins its Class. McClaren

169 'New Greatness' (A IC PR, Bruidegom, 1972, Holland) was introduced as a semi-cactus and changed to an incurved cactus in 1976. It is an easy dahlia to grow on a healthy plant. Wins its Class and Cream of the Crop. Dick Ambrose

170 'Camano Prospero' (A IC LB Y/L, R. Ambrose, 1991, USA) is a blend of yellow with lavender. Both the form of the petals and the depth of the bloom are excellent. It is an easy flower to grow and likes cool humid climates. Wins in a very competitive Class. Dick Ambrose

169 'H G Chad E' (A C PR, R. Jones, 2000, USA) is outstanding with excellent form and full petalage—a flower for all growers of large-sized dahlias. Strong stems and striking color, which deepens as the season progresses, make it a valuable cut and show flower. Does well throughout the United States and Canada. Wins its Class, Best A Cactus in Show, and Cream of the Crop. McClaren

170 'Camano Messenger' (A IC LB PK/Y, R. Ambrose, 1991, USA). Derrill W. Hart Award. This is a blend of pastel pink and yellow with great form and full petalage. Grows and shows well throughout the United States and Canada. Wins its Class, Best A in Show, Best Cactus in Show, Best Bloom in Show, Cream of the Crop, and Fabulous Fifty. S. McClaren

170 'Mingus Gregory' (A IC LB L/W, Mingus, 1997, USA), a good form and an attractive blend, was reclassified from a semi-cactus to an incurved cactus in 2001. It is easy to grow on a healthy plant with early blooms. Wins in a very competitive Class and Best A Incurved Cactus in Show. McClaren

170 'Mingus Julie M' (A C LB PK/W, Mingus, 2000*, USA) is a striking blend of bright pink and white. It shows well on the west coast of Canada and the United States and will do well in other areas as it is more widely distributed. Wins in a very competitive Class. McClaren

171 'Bronze Fashion' (A IC BR, Almand, 1977, USA), an early Jack Almand introduction, has been shown throughout the United States and Canada. It grows well with humidity and cool weather. Wins its Class. S. McClaren

175 'Reiryuu' (A IC BI W/PR, Konishi, 2004, Japan) is a unique bicolor incurved cactus, purple with white tips—the only flower in its class. It is easy to grow on a healthy plant, and the blooms are held erect on tall straight stems. Great as a cut, arranging, and show flower. Yusaku Konishi

181 'Andriana' (A LC W, Freitas, 1987, USA) was shown as a semi-cactus before the laciniated class was established in 1993, when it was reclassified. It has deep laciniated petals and full petalage. Easy to grow and does well in cool humid climates. Wins its Class, Best Laciniated in Show, Best A in Show, Best Bloom in Show, Cream of the Crop, and Fabulous Fifty. S. McClaren

182 'Encore' (A LC Y, Swan Island Dahlias, 2002, USA), a sport of 'Show 'N' Tell' with many of the same characteristics, is a glowing golden yellow with laciniated petals and excellent substance and depth. Wins its Class, Best A Laciniated in Show, Best Laciniated in Show. Swan Island Dahlias

190 'Poetic' (A LC LB W/PK, Bruidegom, 1965, Holland) is a blend of white in the center to a lavender-pink blend in the margins. It is an easy plant to grow with excellent tuber production and many early blooms. Introduced as an A incurved cactus but changed in 1970 to either an incurved cactus or laciniated, and in 1993 to its present classification. Wins in both classes, Best A Incurved Cactus in Show, Best Laciniated in Show, Best A in Show, Cream of the Crop, and Fabulous Fifty. Ben Bartel

193 'Show 'N' Tell' (A LC DB R/Y, Almand, 1985, USA). Derrill W. Hart Award. This dahlia, one of Almand's greatest introductions, was originally classified as a semi-cactus but reclassified when the laciniated class was created—and continued winning. Its color is striking on the show table and in the garden. Wins its Class, Best Laciniated in Show, Best A in Show, Best Bloom in Show, Cream of the Crop, and Fabulous Fifty. Ben Bartel

CHAPTER 3

B Size

THE ADS CLASSIFIES DAHLIAS from 6 to 8 in. (15 to 20 cm) as B. Originally the B classification included all dahlias from 4 to 8 in. (10 to 20 cm). The B class became large enough to split into two classes, 4 to 6 in. (10 to 15 cm) became BB, and 6 to 8 in. (15 to 20 cm) became B. There are currently over 300 varieties of B dahlias, making it the second-largest class after the BB.

The B class does have the greatest number of laciniated dahlias with over 100 varieties; numbers for the very popular laciniateds have increased faster than any other form. The many excellent show flowers in the B class are used extensively in baskets and as cut flowers.

The photos in this chapter represent the 15 color classes and include examples of the formal decorative, informal decorative, semi-cactus, straight cactus, incurved cactus, and laciniated forms.

B PHOTOS

201 'Center Court' (B FD W, Swan Island Dahlias, 1994, USA) is clean white with full petalage. It is easy to grow on a very tall, healthy, well-branched plant. Strong straight stems make it an excellent cut flower for large displays.
Swan Island Dahlias

201 'Lady Liberty' (B FD W, Swan Island Dahlias, 2003, USA) is clean white with pointed petals that roll to the stem. It grows on a healthy plant and is easy to grow. Wins in a very competitive Class.
Swan Island Dahlias

202 'Edna C' (B FD Y, Comstock, 1968, USA). Lynn B. Dudley, Derrill W. Hart, and Stanley Johnson awards. Among the most popular dahlias grown in the United States and Canada, 'Edna C' was classified in 1987 as an A; otherwise, it has been in the B size. When grown to perfection, it is the perfect flower; in cool humid climates it can reach an A size. Wins its Class, Best B Formal Decorative in Show, Best B in Show, Best Bloom in Show, Cream of the Crop, and Fabulous Fifty. McClaren

201 'Evelyn Foster' (B FD W, Foster, 1971, USA), a clean white with excellent form, still scores in shows and is an outstanding cut flower. Does best in the western United States and Canada. Wins its Class, Best B in Show, Best Bloom in Show, and Cream of the Crop. McClaren

202 'Brooke Nicole' (B FD Y, Swan Island Dahlias, 1990, USA) is a very pale yellow with full petalage that does not fade or burn. Well-proportioned stems on a tall healthy plant make it a good cut flower. Swan Island Dahlias

203 'Caproz Arlene's Special' (B FD OR, Probizanski, 2002, USA) is clear orange with full petalage. It will light up the dahlia patch. S. McClaren

203 'Jamboree' (B FD OR, Swan Island Dahlias, 1993, USA) is reddish orange and easy to grow. An attractive garden flower. Swan Island Dahlias

203 'Mrs. Eileen' (B FD OR, Benke, 1988, Germany) is bright dark orange with excellent form and full petalage. It has been grown and shown throughout the United States and Canada and is an attractive addition to a fall dahlia bouquet. Wins its Class. S. McClaren

204 'Jersey's Beauty' (B FD PK, Waite, 1924, USA), a blend of pinks with pleated petals, is one of the oldest dahlias still being grown and shown. Easy to grow on a healthy floriferous plant, it is used as a cut and garden flower. It set the standard for formal decorative blooms in shows and still wins its Class. McClaren

204 'Kenora Lisa' (B FD PK, Leroux, 1990, USA), another excellent show flower hybridized by Gordon Leroux of Washington State, has dominated its class since its introduction. It has perfect salmon-pink petals and full petalage with excellent form. Easy to grow, blooms early, makes a great cut flower, and tolerates heat. Wins its Class, Best of B Formal Decorative, Best B in Show, Best Bloom in Show, Cream of the Crop, and Fabulous Fifty. Ben Bartel

205 'Canby Centennial' (B FD DP, Swan Island Dahlias, 1994, USA) is deep reddish rose with an outline of white on each petal. Easy to grow on a healthy plant, and a good cut and show flower. Wins its Class and Best B in Show.
Swan Island Dahlias

205 'Scaur Swinton' (B FD DP, E. Wilson, 1998, UK) is dark pink with full petalage recurving to the stem. It grows and shows well in the eastern United States and Canada. When introduced it was classified as an informal decorative but reclassified as a formal decorative in 2002. Wins its Class, Best B Formal Decorative, Best B in Show, and Cream of the Crop. Ben Bartel

206 'Caproz Jerry Garcia' (B FD R, Probizanski, 1997, USA) is old rose, a color I've never seen before in dahlias, very different from most reds. Does well in the heat and is an attractive show, garden, and bouquet flower. Wins its Class and Cream of the Crop. McClaren

207 'Alpen Velvet' (B FD DR, McClaren, 1999, USA) has good petal count, excellent form, and a striking red color that does not fade. It is easy to grow throughout the United States and Canada, with many large tubers that keep well in storage. Wins its Class. McClaren

208 'Brian R' (B FD L, Traff, 1995, USA). Derrill W. Hart Award. The flower is a clean lavender with perfect petals and full petalage. Many early blooms are borne on a healthy plant upon strong straight stems. It is easy to grow throughout the United States and Canada and produces many tubers. Tolerates heat. A perfect show and cut flower. Wins its Class, Cream of the Crop, and Fabulous Fifty. McClaren

206 'Robert Lee' (B FD R, Swan Island Dahlias, 2001, USA), a sport of 'Swan's Glory' with many of the same characteristics, is nonfading orange-red with a reverse of yellow on the tips of the pointed petals, which show in the center of the bloom. Easy to grow on a healthy plant. Good substance makes it a valuable cut flower. Swan Island Dahlias

207 'CG Raven' (B FD DR, Larkin/Zydner, 2002, USA) is a nonfading dark red of outstanding form, with perfect petals, full petalage, and strong stems. It is easy to grow and a perfect cut flower, with great potential as a show flower. Wins its Class. S. McClaren

209 'Purple Joy' (B FD PR, Ray, 1959*, Australia) has wide pointed petals and full petalage recurving to the stem. It grows on a healthy plant with many blooms; first blooms tend to be on short stems. A consistent winner since its introduction. Wins its Class, Best B Formal Decorative in Show, Best B in Show, Best Bloom in Show, and Cream of the Crop. Ben Bartel

210 'Miss Delilah' (B FD LB W/PK, Swan Island Dahlias, 2002, USA) is hot pink blending to white in the center with pointed petals. It grows on a strong healthy plant with many blooms and great stems, making it a valuable cut flower. Swan Island Dahlias

211 'Swan's Gold Medal' (B FD BR, Swan Island Dahlias, 1985, USA) is bronze blending to a light bronze in the center with petals rolling to the stem. It is easy to grow on a healthy plant, well branched, with many blooms on strong stems. Swan Island Dahlias

215 'A La Mode' (B FD BI OR/W, Swan Island Dahlias, 1993*, USA) is a clean bicolor of pumpkin-orange and white that doesn't burn on the back. It is easy to grow, with good petal form, full petalage, and abundant tuber production; tends to be a small B size in some areas. A favorite garden flower. Wins in a competitive Class. McClaren

210 'Swan's Glory' (B FD LB Y/OR, Swan Island Dahlias, 1991, USA) is orange blending to yellow on the tips and edges of the pointed petals. It is easy to grow, a healthy plant with strong stems. Swan Island Dahlias

212 'Swan's Olympic Flame' (B FD R, Swan Island Dahlias, 1985, USA) is a bright orange-red with some yellow showing on the reverse tips, giving it a flame appearance. It grows on a healthy plant and is an attractive garden flower. Wins its Class. Swan Island Dahlias

215 'Duet' (B FD BI DR/W, Scott, 1955, USA), a dark red with white tips and full petalage, is a favorite in the garden. It is easy to grow on a healthy plant with good tuber production. Wins its Class, Best B Bicolor in Show, Best Bicolor in Show, People's Choice, Cream of the Crop, and Fabulous Fifty. Ben Bartel

215 'Patches' (B FD BI PR/W, Swan Island Dahlias, 1986, USA) is a striking bicolor with evenly marked white tips. Many blooms are borne on a tall healthy plant. A great cut flower. Wins its Class, Best B Bicolor, and Best Bicolor in Show. Swan Island Dahlias

215 'Ryan C' (B FD BI PR/W, Swan Island Dahlias, 1993, USA) is another white-tipped bicolor; as with other bicolors, it often produces blooms of a solid velvety purple. Many flowers are carried on a tall healthy plant. Wins its Class. Swan Island Dahlias

215 'Seisoh' (B FD BI W/PR, Konishi, 2004, Japan) is a bicolor, white with purple tips, with excellent petal form and full petalage. It is an easy flower to grow and makes an attractive basket and cut flower. Wins its Class. Yusaku Konishi

221 'B J Beauty' (B ID W, Clarke, 1977, UK) has excellent petal form and full petalage. It is easy to grow with long straight stems. Wins its difficult Class. Dick Ambrose

221 'G W's Cody' (B ID W, Wolfe, 2000, USA) is clean clear white with excellent petal form and full petalage. It blooms early and has excellent tuber production. Does well in all climates and tolerates heat. An excellent cut flower with great substance and an all-around flower for the dahlia grower. Wins its very competitive Class. McClaren

221 'Yuukyu' (B ID W, Tokunaga, 1974*, Japan) is clean white with perfect petal form and full petalage recurving to the stem. It is easy to grow on a healthy plant with many blooms on strong stems. Wins in a very competitive Class, Best B Informal Decorative in Show, Best B in Show, and Cream of the Crop. Ben Bartel

222 'Hamari Sunshine' (B ID Y, Ensum, 1996, UK), a yellow with excellent petal form, shows well in the eastern and midwestern United States. Wins its difficult Class, Cream of the Crop, and Fabulous Fifty. Jim Rowse

222 'Masurat Seedling' (B ID Y, Masurat, USA), a clean pastel yellow, has great petal form and outstandingly full petalage with the ray florets curving back to the stem. Should win its Class.
S. McClaren

224 'Helen Richmond' (B ID PK, Swan Island Dahlias, 1998*, USA) is hot pink with notched petals. With excellent depth, full petalage, and long straight stems, it is both a show flower and a good cut flower. Wins its Class, Best Informal Decorative in Show, and Cream of the Crop. Swan Island Dahlias

222 'Lemon Kiss' (B ID Y, Swan Island Dahlias, 1993, USA) is a pastel lemon-yellow with large petals. It is easy to grow on a healthy sturdy plant with an abundance of blooms. Swan Island Dahlias

223 'Hot Number' (B ID OR, Bruidegom, 1970, Holland), a bright orange, is an old favorite. Great stems and substance make it a good cut flower. It is easy to grow on a healthy plant, well branched, with many early blooms.
Dick Ambrose

225 'Tickled Pink' (B ID DP, Swan Island Dahlias, 1967, USA) is dark pink with large petals blended with soft yellow in the center. It is easy to grow on a tall healthy plant and a good cut and show flower. Wins its Class. Swan Island Dahlias

229 'Jennifer's Wedding' (B ID PR, Swan Island Dahlias, 2002, USA) is a dark rich purple with notched petals, giving it a lacy appearance. It is easy to grow on a tall healthy plant with full petalage. Strong straight stems make it an excellent cut and show flower. Wins its Class. Swan Island Dahlias

229 'Suffolk Punch' (B ID PR, Flood, 1975, UK), in shades of purple, is an attractive garden flower, but it lacks petal count in ray florets and therefore sufficient depth for shows. It is easy to grow in all areas with strong straight stems. Wins its Class, Best B Informal Decorative, and Cream of the Crop. Global Publishing

229 'Ripples' (B ID PR, Swan Island Dahlias, 1999, USA), a sport of 'Rip City', is a very dark velvety purple, nearly black. Blooms grow on a healthy lush plant on strong stems—a valuable cut flower. Swan Island Dahlias

230 'April Dawn' (B ID LB L/W, L. Connell, 1984, USA). Lynn B. Dudley, Derrill W. Hart, and Stanley Johnson awards. This dahlia offers a great color blend with perfect petal form and excellent petal count. Grows and shows well wherever the informal decorative is shown. Wins its Class, Best Informal Decorative in Show, Best B in Show, Best Bloom in Show, Cream of the Crop, and Fabulous Fifty. McClaren

230 'Silhouette' (B ID LB Y/L, Swan Island Dahlias, 1996, USA) is ivory-yellow blending to a thin burgundy outlining each petal. It has full petalage, and the blooms are on a healthy strong plant. An unusual color and a valuable cut and show flower. Wins its Class and Best B Informal Decorative in Show.
Swan Island Dahlias

231 'Sundown' (B ID BR, Swan Island Dahlias, 1995, USA) is a great peach-bronze blending to light bronze with pointed well-arranged petals and full petalage. Blooms are carried on strong straight stems on a very tall, healthy, fully branched plant. Swan Island Dahlias

233 'Fidalgo Splash' (B ID DB PR/W, Matthies, 1972, USA) is a dark blend that continues to show off in the garden and on the show bench. It is an easy dahlia to grow on a healthy plant with good tuber production. Wins its Class, People's Choice, and Cream of the Crop.
Ben Bartel

230 'Veca Lucia' (B ID LB L/W, Paradise, 1997, USA) is an attractive blend with full petalage. Grows and shows well on the west coast of Canada and the United States where the temperature is mild and the humidity is high. Wins its difficult Class and Cream of the Crop. S. McClaren

232 'Neon Splendor' (B ID FL, Swan Island Dahlias, 1987, USA) is red-orange blending to orange in the center with well-formed pointed petals and full petalage recurving to the stem. Consistently wins its Class, Best B Informal Decorative in Show and Best B in Show.
Swan Island Dahlias

233 'Normandy Lisanne' (B ID DB R/Y, Schwinck, 1998, USA), a blend of red and yellow, is easy to grow in all areas of the United States. It has full petalage with many well-formed twisted petals with good depth. Wins its Class and Cream of the Crop. Alan Fisher

233 'Who Dun It' (B ID DB PR/W, Swan Island Dahlias, 2000, USA) is pure white blending to a hot fuchsia on the edge of the evenly spaced petals. Easy to grow on a tall healthy plant that tolerates heat, and valuable as a cut flower, especially in large arrangements and baskets. Swan Island Dahlias

235 'Bert Pitt' (B ID BI DR/W, Palminteri, 1974,USA) is a bicolor of dark red with white tips. It is easy to grow, well branched, with many early blooms, and has excellent tuber production; tubers keep well in storage. Tolerates heat; does well in midwestern and eastern United States and continues to win in all areas. Wins its Class, Best Informal Decorative in Show, Best Bicolor in Show, and Cream of the Crop. McClaren

234 'Yellow Harlequin' (B ID V Y/R, Gregersdal, 1998, Denmark), with its eye-catching variegation of bright red and yellow, is a popular cut flower and attractive in the garden, a viewer's favorite. It is an early bloomer, easy to grow on a strong healthy plant with good tuber production. Wins its Class but lacks petals for a full formation. Jim Rowse

234 'Anna' (B ID V W/R, Gregersdal, 1996, Denmark) is white with evenly spaced red markings. It is easy to grow on a tall healthy plant with many early blooms. The small tubers keep well in storage. Wins its Class and Best Variegated in Show. Ben Bartel

241 'Klondike' (B SC W, Redd, 1992, USA). Lynn B. Dudley Award. This clean white was introduced as an A semi-cactus and changed to a B semi-cactus in 1995—both very competitive classes. Given high humidity and cool weather, it is easy to grow on a strong healthy plant with great stems. Wins its Class, Best Semi-Cactus in Show, Best Bloom in Show, Best Triple in Show, Cream of the Crop, and Fabulous Fifty. ADS slide library

242 'Hamari Accord' (B SC Y, Ensum, 1986, UK). Stanley Johnson Award. This dahlia, a clean clear medium yellow, is the standard for semi-cactus petal formation, with a perfect 45° bloom position. It is easy to grow on a healthy fully branched plant with strong straight stems and many blooms. The tubers are well formed and survive long storage. It has won throughout the world since its introduction and more awards during the 1990s than any other dahlia in the United States and Canada. Wins Cream of the Crop and Fabulous Fifty. McClaren

241 'Magic Moment' (B SC W, L. Connell, 1983, USA). Stanley Johnson Award. Always one of the top show dahlias in the United States and Canada, 'Magic Moment' is difficult to beat on the show table. It is easy to grow everywhere, with perfect petal form, full petalage, and a clean white color, often with a blush of lavender if grown in partial shade. Tolerates heat. It is a great flower for the beginning dahlia grower, for the show table or as a cut flower. Wins its very competitive Class, Best Semi-Cactus in Show, Best Bloom in Show, Cream of the Crop, and Fabulous Fifty. Alan Fisher

242 'Campos Hush' (B SC Y, Campobello Dahlia Farms, 1992, USA) has excellent petal form and full petalage of a clean clear ivory. It is easy to grow with good tuber production. Wins its very competitive Class. McClaren

242 'Happy Face' (B SC Y, Swan Island Dahlias, 1974, USA) is a bright clear yellow with full petalage. It grows on a healthy plant with many early blooms on strong stems. A great garden and cut flower. Wins its very competitive Class. Swan Island Dahlias

242 'Kenora Canada' (B SC Y, Leroux, 1987, USA). Derrill W. Hart and Lynn B. Dudley awards. This clean pure bright yellow dahlia has perfectly formed petals and full petalage recurving to the stem. Many perfect blooms are borne on strong straight stems on a sturdy plant. Wins its very competitive Class, Best B Semi-Cactus, Best B in Show, Best Triple in Show, Cream of the Crop, and Fabulous Fifty. ADS slide library

244 'Sweet Dreams' (B SC PK, Swan Island Dahlias, 1993, USA) is a bright clear pastel pink. Many early blooms of firm substance are carried on a healthy plant. Easy to grow and an excellent cut flower. Wins its Class and Cream of the Crop. Ben Bartel

245 'Coral Gypsy' (B SC DP, Swan Island Dahlias, 1996, USA) is rich deep coral-pink. Many well-matched blooms are produced on a tall healthy plant. Striking color and strong stems make it a valuable cut and show flower. Wins its Class. Swan Island Dahlias

247 'Jeanne Gervais' (B SC DR, Redd, 1991, USA) is nonfading dark red with split petals and full petalage recurving to the stem. It is easy to grow with many blooms and good tuber production. Wins its Class, Best B Semi-Cactus in Show, Best B in Show, and Cream of the Crop. ADS slide library

242 'Ruskin Avenger' (B SC Y, Pennington, 1978, UK) is bright clear yellow with perfect petal form and full petalage. All blooms are the same size and form, so it shows well in multiple blooms and baskets. Wins in a very competitive Class. Dick Ambrose

247 'Zapf's Desert Storm' (B SC DR, Zapf, 1992, USA) is brilliant dark red with well-formed petals and full petalage. Many matched blooms are borne on a tall healthy plant on strong straight stems. Grows and shows well in the midwestern United States. Useful as a cut and show flower. Wins its Class, Best B Semi-Cactus, and Cream of the Crop. McClaren

248 'Mingus Louis' (B SC L, Mingus, 2001, USA) offers pinkish lavender blends with full petalage. It grows on a healthy plant with many perfect blooms on strong stems, making it a valuable cut and show flower. Wins its Class. ADS slide library

249 'Geri Scott' (B SC PR, G. Farrier, 1970, USA) is a dark purple with light reverse, visible as a tiny white tip. It lacks petalage, and the first blooms have short stems. Wins its Class. McClaren

248 'Lavender Fantasy' (B SC L, L. Connell, 1991, USA) is pink-lavender blends on petals with some twisting. An attractive garden flower. Wins its Class and Best B Semi-Cactus in Show. ADS slide library

248 'Mingus Tracy Lynn' (B SC L, Mingus, 1997, USA) is a clean lavender with silver tips. Strong stems and firm substance make it an excellent cut flower. Wins its Class. McClaren

250 'Camano Denali' (B SC LB PK/Y, R. Ambrose, 2000, USA), a blend with excellent form and full petalage, is among the highest scorers in its very competitive class. Wins its Class, Best Semi-Cactus in Show, Best B in Show, Best Bloom in Show, Cream of the Crop, and Fabulous Fifty. The future is bright for this dahlia. Alan Fisher

250 'Candy Keene' (B SC LB W/PK, Clarke, 1976, UK) is clean bright pink with perfect form and full petalage. It is not an easy dahlia to grow, but given cool weather with high humidity, the flowers are perfect. Produces very few tubers. Wins in a very competitive Class and Cream of the Crop. Dick Ambrose

250 'Falcon's Future' (B SC LB R/Y, Peck, 1995*, USA). Wins its Class with a very different blend of a pastel old rose blending to a pale yellow. It has a good form and is easy to grow on a healthy plant, but it needs shade and prefers cool weather. McClaren

250 'Gibby Huston' (B SC LB Y/OR, Huston, 1991, Canada) is a bright yellow blending, often with some unevenness, to orange in the margins. It was classified as an A semi-cactus until 1997, when it was changed to a B semi-cactus—both very competitive classes. Wins its Class, Best B Semi-Cactus in Show, and Best B in Show. ADS slide library

250 'Claire Hicks' (B SC LB W/PR, Lundgren, 1977, USA) is white blending to a reddish purple with some irregularities in the petal form. It grows on a healthy plant with good tuber production. Wins in a very competitive Class and Best B Semi-Cactus in Show. ADS slide library

250 'Fine Blend' (B SC LB Y/OR, Bruidegom, 1976, Holland) is a blend of pastel yellow and reddish orange with twirled petals. Wins in a very competitive Class. Dick Ambrose

250 'Grenador Pastelle' (B SC LB OR/Y, Carrington, 1988*, UK), a bright yellow in the center blending to a clean pale orange in the margin, has perfect form with full petalage recurving to the stem. Wins in a very competitive Class, Best B Semi-Cactus in Show, Best B in Show, Best Bloom in Show, and Cream of the Crop. ADS slide library

250 'Jennifer Lynn' (B SC LB Y/PK, Swan Island Dahlias, 1980, USA) is bright pink blending to a touch of yellow on each notched petal. It grows on a tall healthy plant with blooms on strong stems, making it a great cut flower. Swan Island Dahlias

250 'Margaret Ellen' (B SC LB L/Y, Swan Island Dahlias, 2000, USA) is ivory blending to a brushstroke of lavender at the end of each petal. The petals are evenly arranged, giving a pleasing appearance similar to its parent, 'Touch of Class'. It grows on a healthy plant with blooms on long straight stems. A great cut flower. Swan Island Dahlias

250 'Muffey' (B SC LB DP/W, Redd, 1995, USA) is clean white blending to a dark pink, with all the petal edges lined in a darker pink and full-notched petalage recurving to the stem. It was reclassified in 1996 from a laciniated to a semi-cactus. Grows and shows well in the midwestern United States. Wins in a very competitive Class, Best Semi-Cactus in Show, Best B in Show, and Cream of the Crop. Alan Fisher

250 'Pink Pastelle' (B SC LB PK/W, Pashley, 1991, UK) is a pleasing blend with excellent form. Easy to grow with good tuber production. Does best in cool weather and high humidity. Wins its difficult Class. McClaren

250 'Primetime' (B SC LB BR/Y, Swan Island Dahlias, 1994, USA) is golden orange blending to a bright clear yellow at the center. It has excellent evenly spaced petals and full petalage that rolls to the stem. Many blooms are carried on strong straight stems on a tall healthy plant. Excellent cut and show flower. Wins in a very competitive Class and Best B Semi-Cactus in Show. Swan Island Dahlias

251 'Suncatcher' (B SC BR, Larkin/ Zydner, 2002, USA) is golden bronze with full petalage and excellent form. It grows on a tall healthy floriferous plant. Wins its Class, Best Semi-Cactus in Show, and Cream of the Crop. Alan Fisher

252 'Fire Magic' (B SC FL, Swan Island Dahlias, 1991, USA) is a very different color of smoky fuchsia blending to mauve in the center of the bloom. Grows on a mid-sized plant and is a good cut flower. Wins its Class. Swan Island Dahlias

253 'Caproz C J' (B SC DB PK/Y, Probizanski, 1998, USA) is a pink and yellow blend with full petalage, making it a welcome addition to the garden. Wins its Class. S. McClaren

253 'Don Brown' (B SC DB R/Y, Brown, 1991, USA) has full petalage, yellow at the base of the petal blending to a bright red at the tips. Does well in the eastern United States and Canada. Wins Best B Dark Blend in Show and Best B in Show. ADS slide library

253 'H G Brandon' (B SC DB Y/R, R. Jones, 1991, USA) is pastel yellow blending to red with pleated petals and full petalage. It is easy to grow on a tall healthy floriferous plant. Strong straight stems and good substance make it a needed cut flower. Wins in a competitive Class. McClaren

254 'Nicaro' (B SC V Y/R, Swan Island Dahlias, 1965, USA) is variegated, a golden yellow background with red markings. It grows on a healthy tall plant on strong straight stems—a cut and show flower. Wins its Class. Swan Island Dahlias

254 'Rolf' (B SC V Y/R, Gregersdal, 1998, Denmark) has the most perfect variegation markings of any dahlia grown. The dots, flecks, and stripes of brilliant red on the bright yellow are evenly spaced throughout the petal, and the florets too are evenly colored. It is an easy dahlia to grow in all areas on a tall healthy plant with good tuber production. Firm substance and long straight stems make it an excellent cut flower. Wins its Class, Best Variegated Bloom in Show, and Cream of the Crop. McClaren

254 'Sparkler' (B SC V R/OR, Swan Island Dahlias, 1988, USA) is red with orange markings. Small blooms are borne on a tall plant. An attractive cut and garden flower. Swan Island Dahlias

261 'Camano Ivory' (B IC W, R. Ambrose, 1989, USA). Derrill W. Hart and Lynn B. Dudley awards. This clear ivory with perfect form is an easy dahlia to grow on a strong healthy plant with many blooms. Wins its Class, Best B in Show, Best Triple B in Show, Best Bloom in Show, Cream of the Crop, and Fabulous Fifty. Dick Ambrose

262 'Clara Almand' (B IC Y, Almand, 1971, USA). Lynn B. Dudley and Derrill W. Hart awards. This very attractive bloom has excellent petal form with great petal count. Wins its Class and Cream of the Crop. Dick Ambrose

261 'Be Icy' (B IC W, Masurat, 1999, USA). Its name fits its size (B) and color (a clean frosty white), and its petals are deeply incurved, a winning formation. Many blooms are carried on a healthy plant with good branching. Tolerates heat and likes humidity. Wins its Class and Cream of the Crop. McClaren

262 'Chimicum Julia' (B IC Y, D. and L. Smith, 2000, USA) is clear clean bright yellow. It has excellent form with adequate petalage and strong stems. Prefers cool weather and humidity. Wins in a very competitive Class. McClaren

262 'Danum Cream' (B C Y, Oscroft Nursery, 1999*, UK) is a clear bright yellow with excellent petal form and full petalage. It is easy to grow on a healthy plant with good branching and many blooms on strong straight stems. Wins in a very competitive Class and Best B Cactus in Show. Alan Fisher

262 'H G Sunrise' (B IC Y, R. Jones, 2000, USA) is clean clear yellow with excellent petal form and full petalage. The petal formation is twisted, making it an attractive flower. Grows on a strong healthy plant with many blooms and tolerates heat. Does well in all areas. Wins its Class and Best Cactus in Show, and with wider distribution it will continue to win. McClaren

263 'Camano Classic' (B IC OR, R. Ambrose, 1981, USA). Lynn B. Dudley Award. This unusually attractive dahlia has twisted petals that are very consistent in form and size. Excellent form with good depth. It is easy to grow on a healthy plant. Wins its Class and Cream of the Crop. McClaren

263 'Lupin Bonnie R' (B IC OR, Morin, 1996, USA) is clean bright orange with excellent form, consistent, without gaps, giving it an overall smooth appearance, and great petal count, recurving to the stem. Wins its Class, Best Incurved Cactus in Show, Best Bloom in Show, and Cream of the Crop. McClaren

262 'Windhaven Highlight' (B IC Y, Romano, 2000, USA). Lynn B. Dudley Award. This dahlia has excellent formation with light twisting in the petals. It grows in all areas on a healthy plant with good floral production. Wins in a very competitive Class and Cream of the Crop. McClaren

263 'Miss A' (B C OR, Hale, 1984, USA), a pale burnt orange, opens with excellent straight cactus form but tends to become semi-cactus in the back of the bloom. Many blooms with sturdy stems are borne on a strong healthy plant. Does well in all climates and tolerates heat. Wins its Class, Best B Cactus in Show, Cream of the Crop, and Fabulous Fifty. McClaren

265 'Camano Twilight' (B IC DP, R. Ambrose, 1985, USA). Derrill W. Hart Award. This dark pink with full petalage is an easy flower to grow with many blooms. Its color makes it a valuable cut flower. Prefers cool weather with high humidity. Wins its Class. McClaren

265 'Pink Parfait' (B C DP, Swan Island Dahlias, 1982, USA) is a bright yet soft dark pink. It is easy to grow on a tall plant with many blooms and straight strong stems. A valuable cut flower. Wins its Class. Swan Island Dahlias

267 'Juanita' (B C DR, Healy, 1951, South Africa) is nonfading dark red with full petalage recurving to the stem. It is easy to grow on a healthy plant with many blooms and an abundance of tubers that keep in storage. Considered one of the best cactus dahlias for more than half a century. Wins its Class, Best B Cactus in Show, Best B in Show, Best Bloom in Show, Cream of the Crop, and Fabulous Fifty. Ben Bartel

268 'Alpen Dylan' (B IC L, McClaren, 1988, USA) is lavender with silver tips and excellent form. Valuable cut flower with great substance and a long shelf life. Stock is difficult to locate. Wins its Class. McClaren

270 'Alfred Grille' (B IC LB Y/PK, Severin, 1965, Germany) is pastel yellow blending to a soft pink. It has perfect petal form with full petalage. It is easy to grow, a healthy plant in all areas with strong straight stems. Consistently wins its very competitive Class, Best B Incurved Cactus in Show, Best Incurved Cactus in Show, Best Bloom in Show, Cream of the Crop, and Fabulous Fifty. Global Publishing

270 'Camano Ariel' (B C LB Y/PK, R. Ambrose, 1990, USA) is a blend of yellow and pink. It is easy to grow on a floriferous healthy plant. Shows well on the west coast of Canada and the United States and grows best with cool weather and high humidity. Wins in a competitive Class and Cream of the Crop. Alan Fisher

270 'G W's Peace' (B C LB L/W, Wolfe, 2000*, USA) is white with well-formed petals blending to lavender tips. It is easy to grow on a healthy 5 ft. (1.5 m) plant with many blooms. Tolerates heat and has firm substance, a popular cut flower. Wins its Class. McClaren

270 'Parkland Skala' (B IC LB Y/DP, Rowse, 1999, USA) is yellow blending to dark pink in the center. Many early blooms are carried on a strong healthy plant with good branching. Great substance, makes an appealing cut flower. Wins its Class. Jim Rowse

272 'Miyako-Bijin' (B C FL, Konishi, 1988, Japan) is a great blend of bright yellow and red with well-formed petals. It is easy to grow on a tall healthy plant with excellent tuber production. Stems are long and straight—an eye-catcher in the garden and on the show table. Wins its Class and Best B Triple in Show. Yusaku Konishi

271 'Susan F' (B IC BR, Furrow, 1978, USA). Lynn B. Dudley Award. This yellow-bronze wins in a competitive Class, but it is difficult to locate stock. McClaren

270 'Lot O' Honey' (B IC LB Y/L, Takeuchi, 1983, USA) is yellow at the base of the petal blending to a lavender-pink toward the tips. It lacks full petalage. Wins in a competitive Class. Ben Bartel

273 'Camano Shadows' (B IC DB PR/W, R. Ambrose, 1990, USA). Lynn B. Dudley Award. This dahlia is white blending to fuchsia on the center and tips of its twisted petals. Does well in all areas of the United States and Canada. Wins Best B Dark Blend in Show, Cream of the Crop, and Fabulous Fifty. Alan Fisher

275 'Koyoh-Bijin' (B IC BI R/W, Konishi, 1994, Japan) is bright red with large white tips completely hiding the red in the bloom margin. Its strong straight stems make it an artistic designer's flower. Does best in cool climates with high humidity. Wins its Class. Yusaku Konishi

281 'Minerva Magic' (B LC W, L. Havens, 2001, USA) is clear clean white with excellent petal form and twisted tips. Shows well in midwestern United States and Canada. Wins its Class, Best Laciniated in Show, Cream of the Crop, and Fabulous Fifty. S. McClaren

282 'Stellyvonne' (B LC Y, Higgo, 1989, South Africa). Derrill W. Hart Award. 'Stellyvonne' has an interesting history: introduced as an A cactus, for several years it had a double classification and was shown as either an A cactus or an A laciniated; it was classified as laciniated when that form was established in 1993; and in 1999 it was again reclassified as a B laciniated. Throughout the changes, 'Stellyvonne' continued to grow well in all climates and temperatures—and win. Wins in a very competitive Class, Best Laciniated in Show, Best Bloom in Show, Cream of the Crop, and Fabulous Fifty. ADS slide library

275 'Namiki-Michi' (B IC BI OR/W, Konishi, 2003, Japan) is dark orange with white tips and well-formed petals recurving to the stem. It grows on a healthy plant with many blooms on strong straight stems. Needed in the class. Wins its Class and Best B Incurved Cactus in Show. Yusaku Konishi

282 'Lois V' (B LC Y, Schoen, 1991, USA), an outstanding show flower since its introduction, is clean bright yellow with perfect form. Grows and shows well in cool climates with high humidity. The tubers have a short storage life, but plants can be propagated from pot tubers—the extra work is well worth the effort. Wins its Class, Best Laciniated B in Show, Best Laciniated in Show, Best Bloom of the Show, Cream of the Crop, and Fabulous Fifty. McClaren

283 'Al Almand' (B LC OR, Almand, 1993, USA) is bright orange with excellent form. Wins its Class, Best Laciniated in Show, and Cream of the Crop. S. McClaren

285 'Kenora Frills' (B LC DP, Leroux, 1996*, USA) is dark pink with excellent form, deeply split petals, and full petalage. It grows well with high humidity and cool weather. Wins its Class and Cream of the Crop. ADS slide library

287 'Piedmont Rebel' (B LC DR, Faust, 1964, USA), a nonfading dark red, almost black, originally classified as an informal decorative, was among the first dahlias to be reclassified as laciniated when the class was established in 1993. Easy to grow and tolerates heat. Does well in the eastern and southern United States. Wins its Class, Best Laciniated in Show, Best Bloom in Show, Cream of the Crop, and Fabulous Fifty. S. McClaren

287 'Northlake Diva' (B LC DR, Surber, 1999, USA) is a clean dark red that prefers cool weather with humidity. A cut and show flower. Wins its Class. McClaren

290 'E L Fawn Z' (B LC LB Y/PK, M. Norman, 2001, USA) is a pleasing blend of yellow and pink with full petalage. It grows well on the west coast of Canada and the United States and will show well when fully distributed. Wins in a very difficult Class. McClaren

286 'My Wife' (B LC R, Mingus, 1996, USA). Derrill W. Hart Award. This excellent nonfading brilliant red grows on a tall healthy plant with strong branching and many early blooms. Does well in all parts of the United States and Canada. Wins its Class, Best Laciniated B in Show, Best Laciniated in Show, Cream of the Crop, and Fabulous Fifty. Alan Fisher

290 'Granny Norman' (B LC LB Y/PK, T. Norman, 2003, USA) is a clean yellow with full petalage blending to pink at the tips. It is easy to grow on a tall healthy plant with many blooms. Strong straight stems make it a good cut and show flower. Wins in a very competitive Class. ADS slide library

290 'Nenekazi' (B LC LB R/PK, Higgo, 1997, South Africa). Derrill W. Hart and Lynn B. Dudley awards. This dahlia, one of Higgo's great introductions, is an appealing blend of red and pink with ideal form, deep split petals, full petalage, and strong straight stems. It is easy to grow in all climates and tolerates heat. Reclassified in 2003 from a BB and continues to win. Wins its Class, Best B Laciniated in Show, Cream of the Crop, and Fabulous Fifty. McClaren

292 'Creekside Volcano' (B LC FL, Killingsworth, 1997, USA) is a fiery flame blend with good form. Easy to grow in all climates on a tall healthy plant with strong straight stems. It produces many tubers and does well in heat. Reclassified in 2003 from a BB, it is a winner in both classes. Wins its Class, Best Laciniated in Show, and Cream of the Crop. McClaren

292 'Pinelands Pixie' (B LC FL, Higgo, 2003, South Africa) is a perfect flame of yellow at the lower base of the petals blending to a brilliant red on the major part of the ray florets. It has excellent form and full petalage recurving to the stem. Easy to grow on a healthy plant. Wins in a competitive Class. ADS slide library

292 'Sandia Fancy Dancer' (B LC FL, Boley, 2000, USA) is bright yellow blending to orange with fully laciniated petals and full petalage. Many blooms are borne on a healthy plant with strong straight stems. Prefers cooler weather with humidity. Wins its Class and Best Laciniated in Show. Stephen L. Boley

295 'Lipstick' (B LC BI Y/R, D. Kent, 1999, UK), a bicolor of yellow with red tips, has deeply laciniated petals and full petalage. It is easy to grow with many early well-formed blooms on healthy plants. The tubers are numerous and keep well in storage. Wins its Class, Best B Laciniated in Show, Best Laciniated in Show, and Cream of the Crop. S. McClaren

CHAPTER 4

BB Size

The ADS classifies dahlias from 4 to 6 in. (10 to 15 cm) as BB. Prior to 1957 all dahlias from 4 to 8 in. (10 to 20 cm) were classified as B. However, since the class had grown so large many dahlia growers felt the smaller 4 to 6 in. (10 to 15 cm) dahlias could not compete at shows with the larger 6 to 8 in. (15 to 20 cm) dahlias, thus the addition of the BB class.

The BB class has the greatest number of varieties. It is especially popular among florists for arrangements, bouquets, and baskets. Home gardeners find the size ideal for a cut flower.

The photos in this chapter represent the 15 color classes and include examples of the formal decorative, informal decorative, semi-cactus, straight cactus, incurved cactus, and laciniated forms.

BB PHOTOS

301 'Alpen Cloud' (BB FD W, McClaren, 2003, USA) is crystal-clear white with blooms of great substance. Easy to grow and produces many tubers that store well. Tolerates heat. An excellent seed parent and a great cut flower. Should win its Class. McClaren

301 'Alpen Steve' (BB FD W, McClaren, 2002, USA). Derrill W. Hart Award. This dahlia offers perfect color and form with full petalage recurving to the stem. Easy to grow in all climates and tolerates heat. Great substance and a long shelf life make it a great show and cut flower. It can grow to a B size and is an outstanding seed parent. Wins in a very competitive Class. McClaren

301 'Pat 'N' Dee' (BB FD W, Pape, 1953, USA) was classified as a ball until 1975, when it was reclassified as a BB. It has great form, clear clean white color, and an abundance of petals on a strong healthy plant. Does well in all areas. Valuable cut flower and an outstanding seed parent. Many competitors have come and gone, but 'Pat 'N' Dee' continues to win its Class and Cream of the Crop. McClaren

301 'White Purity' (BB FD W, L. Connell, 1991, USA) is white with full petalage. Does well in cool weather and humidity and has proven itself as a cut flower. Wins its Class. McClaren

302 'Lemon Shiffon' (BB FD Y, Swan Island Dahlias, 1998, USA) is delicate soft yellow. It is easy to grow on healthy plants with many early blooms. The stems are straight and long, making it an excellent cut and arranging flower. Swan Island Dahlias

302 'Ruskin Diane' (BB FD Y, Pennington, 1984, UK) is a clear bright yellow with perfect petal form and full petalage recurving to the stem. It grows on a tall plant with many perfect blooms. Does best in high humidity, cool weather, and shade. Wins its competitive Class, Best BB Formal Decorative in Show, Best BB in Show, Best Bloom in Show, Cream of the Crop, and Fabulous Fifty. McClaren

303 'David Digweed' (BB FD OR, Davies, 1995, UK) is light bronze-orange with many perfect petals recurving to the stem. Easy to grow. Does well in cool climates with humidity. It was classified as a ball until 2000 and wins in both classes, Best BB in Show, and Best Bloom in Show. S. McClaren

303 'Long Island Lil' (BB FD OR, Wicks, 1993, USA). Lynn B. Dudley Award. This dahlia is easy to grow in all climates and tolerates heat. Many blooms are carried on a strong healthy plant, with excellent early blooms for cut flowers. Wins its Class and Cream of the Crop. McClaren

304 'Cuddles' (BB FD PK, Swan Island Dahlias, 1989, USA) is bright pink with a scattering of semi-cactus petals. It is easy to grow on a healthy plant with many blooms of great substance. Its attractive color makes it an excellent cut flower. Swan Island Dahlias

303 'Jomanda' (BB FD OR, Geerlings, 1996, Holland) is a deep bright orange with full petalage and grows well in all areas. It was classified as a ball until 2000. Wins its Class, Best BB in Show, Best Bloom in Show, Cream of the Crop, and Fabulous Fifty. McClaren

304 'Barbary Dominion' (BB FD PK, Davies, 1989, UK) is soft pastel pink with outstanding form and full petalage. It is easy to grow in all climates, tolerates heat, and produces excellent tubers. Classified as a miniature until 1999 and wins in both classes. Wins its Class, Best BB in Show, Best Bloom in Show, Cream of the Crop, and Fabulous Fifty. McClaren

304 'Hillcrest Kismet' (BB FD PK, Jackson, 2000*, UK), a salmon-pink with full petalage and great form, quickly became a winner. Easy to grow, it blooms early and prolifically, with perfectly matched flowers, on a tall healthy plant with straight, strong stems. Does well in all areas of the United States. Wins in a very competitive Class and Cream of the Crop. ADS slide library

304 'Intrigue' (BB FD PK, Swan Island Dahlias, 2002, USA) is a salmon-pink with well-formed formal decorative petals. Does well in cool humid conditions. Its blooms have good substance and are on strong straight stems, making it a popular cut and arranging flower. Swan Island Dahlias

305 'Skipley Mii Too' (BB FD DP, R. Williams, 1999, USA) is dark pink with many petals and excellent form. It is easy to grow on a healthy plant with excellent stems and good tuber production. Wins its Class and Best BB in Show. McClaren

305 'Triple Lee D' (BB FD DP, Duxbury, 1998, Canada) is dark pink with perfect petal formation and great form. Easy to grow and produces excellent tubers. Wins its Class and Cream of the Crop. Always a winner. McClaren

304 'Netterbob' (BB FD PK, Swan Island Dahlias, 2001, USA), a deep pink, is easy to grow on a healthy floriferous plant. Great stems for cutting. Swan Island Dahlias

305 'Tempest' (BB FD DP, Swan Island Dahlias, 1997, USA), a coral-pink with well-arranged pointed petals, grows on a healthy plant. Adds a great color to bouquets and fall arrangements. Wins its Class. Swan Island Dahlias

306 'Barbarry Intrepid' (BB FD R, Davies, 2003, UK). Lynn B Dudley Award. This brilliant sparkling red, with perfectly formed pointed petals and full petalage recurving to the stem, has all the characteristics of a Davies introduction. Its form and color make it a show and cut flower. Wins in a very competitive Class. ADS slide library

306 'Creekside Betty' (BB FD R, Killingsworth, 2001, USA) is bright nonfading red with a yellow reverse, well-formed pointed petals, and full petalage recurving to the stem. Easy to grow and tolerates heat. An attractive garden flower. Wins in a very competitive Class. ADS slide library

307 'Barbarry Strand' (BB FD DR, Davies, 2002, UK), a nonfading dark red, is another of Davies's attractive formal decorative forms, with an abundance of perfectly formed petals. Wins in a very competitive Class. McClaren

307 'Danjo Doc' (BB FD DR, Docherty, 1996, UK) is nonfading very dark red, nearly black. The form is full with many perfect petals. Wins in a very competitive Class and Cream of the Crop. S. McClaren

306 'Mingus Kyle D' (BB FD R, Mingus, 1996, USA) is a light purplish red. It is easy to grow on a tall healthy plant with many blooms. Does well in all areas of the United States and Canada. Wins in a very competitive Class. McClaren

307 'Black Satin' (BB FD DR, Swan Island Dahlias, 1995, USA) is dark red. It grows on a tall healthy plant with many blooms. Excellent cut flower with strong straight stems and firm substance. Wins in a very competitive Class and Best BB in Show. Swan Island Dahlias

307 'Parkland Midnight' (BB FD DR, Rowse, 1995, USA) is nonfading dark red. It is easy to grow on a tall healthy plant. Excellent cut flower with strong straight stems. Wins in a very competitive Class. Jim Rowse

307 'Ruby Slippers' (BB FD DR, Swan Island Dahlias, 2003, USA) is dark ruby-red with petals rolling to the stem. It has dark mahogany foliage, which is a great contrast to the color of the bloom. With its excellent form and color, it wins in a very competitive Class.
Swan Island Dahlias

307 'Swan's Discovery' (BB FD DR, Swan Island Dahlias, 1990, USA) is dark red, nearly black. It makes a very successful border plant in landscapes and grows well in pots on the patio. Wins in a very competitive Class. Swan Island Dahlias

308 'Camano Choice' (BB FD L, R. Ambrose, 1981, USA). Derrill W. Hart Award. One of the outstanding dahlias of the last quarter century, 'Camano Choice' is easy to grow on a healthy plant with many early blooms. The form is perfect, with attractively pleated petals, and the color an eye-catching shimmering soft lavender. It wins everything possible: Best in its Class, Best BB in Show, Best Bloom in Show, Cream of the Crop for many years, and Fabulous Fifty.
Dick Ambrose

307 'Smarty Pants' (BB FD DR, Swan Island Dahlias, 2001, USA) is dark red with well-arranged petals and deep dark foliage. Many blooms are borne on long straight stems on a healthy low-growing plant. Excellent border plant for landscapes, useful for cut flowers, and, with its compact growth, a great patio plant.
Swan Island Dahlias

307 'Voodoo' (BB FD DR, Swan Island Dahlias, 2000, USA) is very dark red, nearly black, with round petals. It is easy to grow on a tall floriferous plant; blooms are held on tall straight stems and have great substance and a long shelf life. Makes a fine contrast in floral designs and bouquets. Swan Island Dahlias

308 'Gala Parade' (BB FD L, T. Morgan, 1996*, New Zealand) has an abundance of lavender petals in correct formation. Wins in a very competitive Class, Best BB in Show, Best Bloom in Show, Cream of the Crop, and Fabulous Fifty. McClaren

308 'Hillcrest Carmen' (BB FD L, Jackson, 1998, UK) is light lavender and white—could be classified as a blend. Wins its Class with excellent form and good stems. McClaren

308 'Rock A Bye' (BB FD L, Swan Island Dahlias, 1999, USA) is lavender with rounded petals. It is easy to grow on a healthy plant with many perfect blooms. Stems are good for cutting. Wins its Class. Swan Island Dahlias

309 'Badger Beauty' (BB FD PR, Senty, 1967, USA) is blends of light purple (it was reclassified in 1976 from lavender to purple) with pleated pointed petals and full petalage. Color is best when grown in semi-shade. An attractive cut and garden flower. Ben Bartel

308 'Molly' (BB FD L, Goff, 2001, USA) is reddish lavender with pointed pleated petals that are uneven in size. It is an unusual color, attractive in the garden. ADS slide library

308 'Stacy Rachelle' (BB FD L, Swan Island Dahlias, 1993, USA) is blends of lavender, darker on the tips of the bloom. It grows on a healthy floriferous plant with strong cutting stems. Wins its Class. Swan Island Dahlias

309 'Irene Ellen' (BB FD PR, Knight, 1999, UK) is very dark reddish purple, nearly black toward the center. It is small and well formed, with a large petal count. Wins in a very competitive Class, Best BB Formal Decorative in Show, and Best BB in Show. ADS slide library

309 'Lupin Chris' (BB FD PR, Morin, 1992, USA) is reddish purple with a lighter reverse, good petal count, and excellent form. Offers many early blooms. Wins its Class, Best Single and Triple BB in Show. McClaren

309 'Rosemarie' (BB FD PR, Powse-Lybbe, 2003, Canada) is rose-purple with perfect petal form and full petalage recurving to the stem. Easy to grow on a healthy well-branched plant. Good substance makes it a valuable cut and show flower. Wins in a very competitive Class. McClaren

310 'Camano Pearl' (BB FD LB W/L, R. Ambrose, 1978, USA) is white with blends of lavender and full petalage. It is easy to grow on a healthy plant with many blooms of good substance held on strong straight stems. A popular cut flower. Wins in a competitive Class. McClaren

309 'Midnight Dancer' (BB FD PR, Swan Island Dahlias, 1992, USA) is very dark reddish purple with a lighter reverse. Its petals have excellent form, being broad and flat. An attractive cut flower with many early blooms. Wins in a very competitive Class. McClaren

309 'Taboo' (BB FD PR, Swan Island Dahlias, 2003, USA), a sport of 'Voodoo', has excellent petal form and full petalage. It grows on a tall healthy plant with strong straight stems. A needed color for cut flowers, and exhibits well in shows. Swan Island Dahlias

310 'Coralie' (BB FD LB W/PK, T. Mantle, 1982, UK) is a blend of pastel pink with white. Its petals are excellently shaped, with good form and full petalage recurving to the stem. Many early blooms with great stems are borne on a healthy plant with good tuber production. An attractive cut flower. Wins in a very competitive Class and Cream of the Crop. McClaren

310 'Hamilton Lillian' (BB FD LB OR/Y, Hamilton, 1986, Canada). Lynn B. Dudley, Derrill W. Hart, and Stanley Johnson awards. This most outstanding dahlia was reclassified in 2000 from an orange to a blend of orange and yellow, and still grows as a solid orange in many areas of the United States. Easy to grow and tolerates heat. Wins its Class, Best Single and Triple BB in Show, Best Bloom in Show, Cream of the Crop, and Fabulous Fifty. ADS slide library

310 'Hy Clown' (BB FD LB Y/BR, W. Holland, 1995, Canada) is yellow blending to dark bronze—nearly a bicolor. Many uniform early blooms are carried on a tall healthy plant. Excellent tuber production. Tolerates heat. Wins its Class, Best BB in Show, Cream of the Crop, and Fabulous Fifty. McClaren

310 'Parkland Heather' (BB FD LB L/W, Rowse, 1996, USA), a reddish lavender blending to white, grows on a tall healthy floriferous plant with many laterals. It is easy to grow with good tuber production. Excellent cut flower. Wins its Class. Jim Rowse

310 'Heather Feather' (BB FD LB W/PK, Swan Island Dahlias, 2002, USA), a soft pink blending to white in the center of the bloom, grows on a tall healthy floriferous plant. Excellent for cut flowers, baskets, and arrangements that require long stems. Swan Island Dahlias

310 'Normandy DeeGee' (BB FD LB PK/Y, Schwinck, 1991, USA). Derrill W. Hart Award. This is a pale yellow dahlia blending to pink, with split-ended petals and full petalage. Wins in a very competitive Class and Best BB Formal Decorative. McClaren

310 'Snickerdoodle' (BB FD LB Y/OR, Swan Island Dahlias, 2000, USA) is yellow blending to orange with a deep rose reverse and evenly spaced petals. It grows on a tall plant that should be topped to develop strong laterals for cutting. Excellent cut flower for fall arrangements. Swan Island Dahlias

310 'Watercolors' (BB FD LB L/W, Swan Island Dahlias, 1997, USA) is pure clean white blending to lavender toward the tips. It grows on a healthy plant with many blooms throughout the season. Swan Island Dahlias

311 'Ferncliff Copper' (BB FD BR, D. Jack, 1990*, Canada) is bronze with pleated petals. Early blooms are carried on a tall healthy plant. It is easy to grow, has excellent tuber production, and tolerates heat. Wins its Class and Cream of the Crop. S. McClaren

313 'Alpen X' (BB FD DB PK/Y, McClaren, 2001, USA) is pink blending to soft yellow with excellent form, flat petals, and full petalage. It is easy to grow on a healthy plant with good tuber production and strong straight stems. Does well in all climates. Tolerates heat. Wins its Class. McClaren

311 'Dustin Williams' (BB FD BR, Swan Island Dahlias, 1997, USA) offers blends of bronze, a necessary color in the garden, with full petalage. It is easy to grow on a well-branched plant with many flowers. Excellent cut and basket flower. Swan Island Dahlias

311 'G W's Rusty' (BB FD BR, Wolfe, 2000, USA) is bright yellow-bronze with flat petals. It is easy to grow with many blooms on strong stems but tends to lack petal count. Valued as a cut. Wins its Class. McClaren

313 'CG Regal' (BB FD DB W/PR, Larkin/Zydner, 2002, USA) is white blending to dark purple petal tips—nearly a bicolor. Easy to grow with good tuber production. Wins its Class. S. McClaren

313 'Sweet Content' (BB FD DB Y/DR, W. Paterson, 1970, UK) is yellow in the margins blending to dark red in the center of the bloom. Easy to grow with many early blooms and good tuber production. Wins its Class, Best BB in Show, and Cream of the Crop. McClaren

314 'G W's Nancy Ann' (BB FD V PK/DR, Wolfe, 1999, USA) is pink with dark red variegations and full petalage. It grows on a tall healthy plant with many early blooms of great substance, making it an excellent cut and show flower. Tolerates heat. Wins in a very competitive Class. McClaren

314 'Vernon Rose' (BB FD V PK/DR, Stowell, 1977, USA). Derrill W. Hart Award. Grown and shown for many years, this is a perfect variegated dahlia with even color and markings, excellent petal form, and full petalage, making it difficult to beat. Wins in a very competitive Class, Best BB in Show, Best Variegated in Show, Cream of the Crop, and Fabulous Fifty. Alan Fisher

314 'Connecticut Dancer' (BB FD V W/DR, C. Jones, 1970, USA) is white with excellent evenly marked dark red variegations and full petalage. It grows in all climates on a tall healthy plant with many early blooms. Wins in a very challenging Class, Best Variegated in Show, Best BB in Show, Cream of the Crop, and Fabulous Fifty. McClaren

314 'Lupin Ben' (BB FD V Y/R, Morin, 1992, USA) is bright yellow with a small number of brilliant red markings. It is easy to grow with many early blooms. Tolerates heat. Wins its very difficult Class and Cream of the Crop. S. McClaren

315 'Angel Face' (BB FD BI R/W, Lammerse, 1961*, Holland), among the earlier bicolors on the show table and in the garden, is red with large white tips and full petalage. Wins its Class. S. McClaren

315 'Brian Ray' (BB FD BI PR/W, Swan Island Dahlias, 1997, USA), a bright purple with evenly marked pointed tips and full petalage, is a perfect bicolor. It grows on a tall healthy plant with blooms on strong wiry stems. Excellent cut flower. Wins its Class. Swan Island Dahlias

315 'Lemon Candy' (BB FD BI Y/W, Swan Island Dahlias, 1995, USA), a sport of 'Candy Cane', is a clear bright yellow with clean white tips. It is easy to grow on a healthy well-branched plant. An eye-catching addition to the garden. Swan Island Dahlias

315 'Magically Dun' (BB FD BI W/R, Swan Island Dahlias 2001*, USA) is a bicolor, white with red tips, with full petalage. Wins in a very competitive Class. S. McClaren

315 'Ringo' (BB FD BI R/W, Swan Island Dahlias, 1994, USA), a deep red with white tips, is carried on a mid-sized plant. Valuable as a border plant, therefore, and a good cut flower. Wins its Class. Swan Island Dahlias

315 'Skipley Spot' (BB FD BI R/W, R. Williams, 1989, USA) is a bicolor with excellent form and color and full petalage. Easy to grow on a strong healthy plant with many early nonfading blooms. It has good tuber production and does well in all climates. Wins its Class, Best BB in Show, Best Bicolor in Show, Cream of the Crop, and Fabulous Fifty. McClaren

315 'Snoho Christmas' (BB FD BI DR/W, Bonneywell, 1995, USA) is an outstanding bicolor, a nonfading dark red with white tips. It is easy to grow on a tall healthy plant with many early blooms and good tuber production. An attractive cut flower with good substance. Wins its Class. McClaren

315 'Tip Toe' (BB FD BI PR/W, Almand, 1972, USA) is another outstanding bicolor, purple with perfect white tips. It grows on a healthy plant, but tubers are difficult to store for long periods. An attractive show and cut flower. Wins its Class. McClaren

315 'Tomo' (BB FD BI PR/W, C. Chilson, 1988*, USA) is reddish purple with uniformly small white tips. The petals are pleated, well formed with full petalage. Valued as a cut flower. Wins in a competitive Class and Best Bicolor in Show. McClaren

321 'Allie White' (BB ID W, Simmons, 1999, USA) is clean white with pleated petals. It grows on a healthy plant with many blooms of great substance on straight stems. Long shelf life makes it an excellent cut flower. Wins its Class, Best BB Informal Decorative in Show, Best Bloom in Show, and Cream of the Crop. ADS slide library

321 'Gitts Attention' (BB ID W, Swan Island Dahlias, 2000, USA). Derrill W. Hart Award. This creamy white dahlia offers notched petals and full petalage. It is easy to grow in all areas on a strong healthy plant. Long shelf life and great stems make it an outstanding cut flower. Wins its Class and Cream of the Crop. Swan Island Dahlias

322 'Bo-De-O' (BB ID Y, Boeke, 1987, USA) is a clean bright yellow. Does well in all areas of the United States and Canada. Wins its Class. S. McClaren

322 'Nick's Pick' (BB ID Y, Swan Island Dahlias, 1997, USA) is bright yellow with a blush of orange and well-formed petals. Many blooms are held on sturdy straight stems on a tall healthy plant. Great cut and arranging flower. Swan Island Dahlias

322 'Parakeet' (BB ID Y, Swan Island Dahlias, 1997, USA) is softest yellow with full petalage. It is easy to grow on a healthy plant with many blooms on strong straight stems. An excellent cut flower. Swan Island Dahlias

324 'Excentric' (BB ID PK, Swan Island Dahlias, 1999, USA) is a bright hot pink with informal decorative intermixed with formal decorative petals. The great stems and attractive color make it a valuable cut flower. Wins its Class. Swan Island Dahlias

324 'Silverado' (BB ID PK, Swan Island Dahlias, 1994, USA) is a soft lilac-pink with a silver sheen. Valuable as a cut flower, it grows on a tall healthy plant, well branched, with many blooms throughout the season. Wins its Class and Best Informal Decorative in Show. Swan Island Dahlias

323 'San Francisco Sunrise' (BB ID OR, Juul, 1998*, USA) is pale orange with excellent petals. It grows and shows well in cool weather with high humidity. Wins its Class and Cream of the Crop. S. McClaren

324 'Lindy' (BB ID PK, Swan Island Dahlias, 1995, USA) is shades of pink throughout the season, depending on weather conditions. Valuable cut and show flower. Wins its Class. Swan Island Dahlias

326 'Serenade' (BB ID R, Swan Island Dahlias, 1997, USA) is orange-red with excellent stems for cut flowers. It grows on a healthy dark-leaved plant with many blooms throughout the season. Swan Island Dahlias

327 'Rip City' (BB ID DR, Swan Island Dahlias, 1992*, USA) is an exotic dark red, nearly black. It is easy to grow with many nonfading blooms. Attracts attention on the show bench and in the garden as a cut flower. Wins its Class.
Swan Island Dahlias

328 'Lavid' (BB ID L, Larkin/Zydner, 1998, USA) is lavender and easy to grow on a strong healthy plant. Excellent stems, good tuber production, keeps well in storage. Wins its Class and Cream of the Crop. S. McClaren

328 'Winter Ice' (BB ID L, Swan Island Dahlias, 1985, USA) is a delicate soft bluish lavender with excellent petal form. It grows on a tall well-branched plant with many blooms. Swan Island Dahlias

328 'Jenna' (BB ID L, Swan Island Dahlias, 1995, USA), a bright rose-pink, blooms prolifically on a tall lush plant. It is a good cut and show flower, especially in late summer. Wins its Class.
Swan Island Dahlias

328 'Seduction' (BB ID L, Swan Island Dahlias, 1998, USA) is attractive blends of dark lavender, running down the center of the petals, with lighter lavender on the edges and a purple reverse. It should be topped for longer stems. Wins its Class and Best Informal Decorative in Show. Swan Island Dahlias

329 'Imperial Wine' (BB ID PR, Swan Island Dahlias, 2000, USA) offers rich nonfading color and notched petals. It grows on a very tall healthy plant with great substance; needs to be topped for good lateral growth. A valuable cut and show flower. Wins its Class and Best Informal Decorative BB in Show. Swan Island Dahlias

330 'Chilson's Pride' (BB ID LB W/PK, C. Chilson, 1954*, USA) is pastel pink blending to white with perfect formation. Early and markedly uniform blooms are carried on a tall healthy floriferous plant. Easy to grow, tolerates heat, and produces excellent tubers that store well. Wins its Class, Best BB in Show, Best Informal Decorative in Show, Cream of the Crop, and Fabulous Fifty. S. McClaren

330 'Gay Princess' (BB ID LB W/PK, Richards, 1975, UK), a blend of pink and white with notched petals, grows on a tall healthy plant with many early blooms. This outstanding and easy-to-grow cut flower has won on the show table under various classifications during its lifetime: formal decorative, informal decorative, waterlily, laciniated, pink, and light blend. Wins its Class, Best BB Informal Decorative in Show, Best BB in Show, Cream of the Crop, and Fabulous Fifty. McClaren

330 'Banana Rama' (BB ID LB Y/L, Swan Island Dahlias, 2001, USA) is soft yellow blending to pastel lavender toward the tips. Healthy foliage and many blooms make it an outstanding garden plant, and its color complements all dahlia arrangements. Swan Island Dahlias

330 'Ed Johnson' (BB ID LB Y/OR, Masurat, 1997*, USA) is pale yellow blending to orange. It grows well on the west coast of North America. Wins in a competitive Class. S. McClaren

332 'Procyon' (BB ID FL, Maarse, 1963, Holland) is an old-time dahlia with bright red petals in the margin of the bloom and a yellow center with small notches on the petals. Easy to grow in all climates. Wins its Class and Cream of the Crop. S. McClaren

333 'Dark Magic' (BB ID DB W/PR, Pollard, 1986*, New Zealand), a deep fuchsia blending to silver tips, grows on a tall healthy plant with many long-lasting blooms. It produces an abundance of tubers that have a good storage life. Attractive on the show bench and one of the outstanding cut flowers sold in the market. Wins its Class, Best Informal Decorative in Show, Best BB in Show, Cream of the Crop, and Fabulous Fifty. McClaren

334 'Pop Talk' (BB ID V L/PR, Bruidegom, 1976, Holland), a lavender with dark purple variegations, is a favorite in the garden as a cut flower and on the show table with its long straight stems. It is easy to grow and produces many tubers that store well. Wins its Class and Cream of the Crop. McClaren

335 'Matchmaker' (BB ID BI W/PR, L. Connell, 1986, USA) is easy to grow on a healthy plant with strong straight stems and great substance—a great cut flower. Wins its Class. S. McClaren

341 'Minerva Misty' (BB SC W, L. Havens, 2001, USA) is white with a slight lavender blush. It has full petalage with some twisted petals. Wins its Class. McClaren

341 'Snowgrandma' (BB SC W, Masurat, 1996, USA). Derrill W. Hart Award. This semi-cactus with blunt petals and full petalage is easy to grow on a strong healthy plant. Good tuber production, tolerates heat. Wins its Class and Cream of the Crop. Alan Fisher

342 'Alpen Mildred' (BB SC Y, McClaren, 1983, USA) is a golden yellow with full petalage and excellent form. It is easy to grow in all climates. Excellent tuber production, tolerates heat. Wins its Class and Best Bloom in Show. McClaren

342 'Pucker Up' (BB SC Y, Swan Island Dahlias, 2002, USA) is a bright lemon-yellow with strong stems for cut flowers. Swan Island Dahlias

342 'Embrace' (BB SC Y, T. Griffin, 1999*, Australia) is a golden yellow with outstanding form and full petalage. It grows throughout the world in all climates. Wins its Class, Best Semi-Cactus in Show, Cream of the Crop, and Fabulous Fifty. ADS slide library

344 'Camano Cloud' (BB SC PK, R. Ambrose, 1978, USA). Lynn B. Dudley Award. This is a great show flower, a clean light pink with excellent formation and full petalage. The plant is floriferous and grows best from pot tubers. Wins its Class, Best BB in Show, Best Flower of Show, Cream of the Crop, and Fabulous Fifty. Dick Ambrose

343 'Tropic Sun' (BB SC OR, Swan Island Dahlias, 1998, USA) is shades of soft orange on strong straight stems carried on a tall healthy plant. It is useful as a cut, basket, show, and designer's flower. Wins its Class. Swan Island Dahlias

342 'Lemon Elegance' (BB SC Y, Geerlings, 1989, Holland) is soft pastel yellow with full petalage and excellent incurved petals recurving to the stem. An easy-to-grow cut and show flower with strong stems. Wins its Class, Best Semi-Cactus in Show, and Cream of the Crop. Alan Fisher

344 'Joy Ride' (BB SC PK, Swan Island Dahlias, 1995, USA), a hot pink, is borne on a healthy plant. Useful as a cut and designer's flower. Swan Island Dahlias

344 'Love Potion' (BB SC PK, Swan Island Dahlias, 1999, USA) is hot pink with excellent petal form and full petalage. It is easy to grow on a healthy plant. Strong stems for cut flowers.
Swan Island Dahlias

345 'Athalie' (BB SC DP, Dawes, 1974, UK) has perfect petal form with full petalage. The color is a striking pink with tiny white tips on each petal. This is an easy flower to grow on a tall healthy fully branched plant with many blooms—a constant winner at shows and a great cut flower since its introduction. Wins its Class, Best Single and Triple BB in Show, Best BB in Show, Best Bloom in Show, Cream of the Crop, and Fabulous Fifty.
ADS slide library

346 'Hi Lite' (BB SC R, Swan Island Dahlias, 1991, USA) is an unusual watermelon-red. Many blooms are carried on a tall healthy plant with sturdy stems for cutting. Swan Island Dahlias

344 'Touché' (BB SC PK, Swan Island Dahlias, 1994, USA) is shades of salmon-pink with a reverse of lavender blush. It grows on a mid-sized plant with many very early blooms and strong stems for cutting. Swan Island Dahlias

345 'Conway' (BB SC DP, Weekes, 1986, UK) is dark salmon-pink with excellent petal form and full petalage. Does well in all areas and is an attractive cut flower. Wins its Class and Cream of the Crop.
McClaren

346 'Obsession' (BB SC R, Swan Island Dahlias, 1998, USA) is a brilliant red with a reverse of white on the tip of the petals. It is an ideal cut flower with excellent stems, particularly valuable for large collections and baskets.
Swan Island Dahlias

347 'Dare Devil' (BB SC DR, Swan Island Dahlias, 1999, USA) is bold dark red with perfect incurved petals and full petalage. It is a great garden flower, easy to grow on a well-branched plant with many blooms. Strong straight stems for cut flowers. Swan Island Dahlias

347 'Taylor Nelson' (BB SC DR, Almand, 1994, USA). Derrill W. Hart Award. This is a tall plant, easy to grow, with many early blooms. Great cut flower. Reclassified in 1996 from an incurved cactus to a semi-cactus, and in some areas it reaches B size. Wins both classes and Cream of the Crop. McClaren

348 'Alice Denton' (BB SC L, Splinter, 1992, USA) is blends of lavender with tiny silver tips and full petalage recurving to the stem. It is easy to grow in all areas on a healthy plant with many blooms on long straight stems. Great substance makes it a valuable cut and show flower. Wins its Class, Best BB Semi-Cactus in Show, and Cream of the Crop. ADS slide library

347 'Oreti Jewel' (BB SC DR, W. Jack, 1999, New Zealand) is dark red with blunt petals, excellent form, and full petalage. It is easy to grow on a tall healthy plant with many perfect blooms on long straight stems, making it a fine cut flower. Wins its Class and Best BB Semi-Cactus in Show. Walter Jack

347 'Vets Love' (BB SC DR, Hanni-Wilcox, 1994, USA), a nonfading dark red, grows on a 6 ft. (1.8 m) healthy plant with many blooms and excellent tuber production. Excellent cut flower. McClaren

348 'Worton Blue Streak' (BB SC L, I. S. Lewis, 1975, UK), a lavender with hints of blue, has evenly spaced petals and full petalage. It is an easy plant to grow with many perfect blooms. Wins in a competitive Class, Best BB in Show, Best Bloom in Show, Cream of the Crop, and Fabulous Fifty. McClaren

349 'Hy Myst' (BB SC PR, W. Holland, 2001*, Canada) is purple with light purple tips, excellent petal form, and full petalage. It grows on a tall healthy floriferous plant. Excellent cut flower. Wins its Class and Cream of the Crop.
S. McClaren

350 'Ballerina' (BB SC LB PK/W, Swan Island Dahlias, 1996, USA) is ivory blending to a soft pink margin with excellent petal form and full petalage. It grows on a healthy fully branched plant with many perfect blooms. Strong straight stems and blooms of great substance make it a perfect cut flower.
Swan Island Dahlias

350 'Gerda Juul' (BB SC LB Y/OR, Juul, 1980, USA) is yellow blending to orange with excellent petal form and full petalage. It is easy to grow on a healthy plant with good tuber production. Its color makes it an outstanding cut flower. Wins in a very competitive Class. Alan Fisher

350 'Alpen Dawn' (BB SC LB Y/PK, McClaren, 2004, USA) is bright yellow blending to pink with full petalage. It is easy to grow on a healthy plant with many early blooms. Strong straight stems make it a valuable cut and show flower. Wins its Class and Best Single BB in Show. McClaren

350 'First Kiss' (BB SC LB W/PK, Swan Island Dahlias, 1995, USA). It is soft clear pink blending to white in the center of the flower with semi-cactus petal form. It grows on a healthy sturdy plant with the blooms having great substance for long-lasting cut flowers.
Swan Island Dahlias

350 'Jil' (BB SC LB L/W, Swan Island Dahlias, 1994, USA), a clean white blending to bright lavender, is borne on strong straight stems on a healthy plant. A good cut and show flower. Wins its Class. Swan Island Dahlias

350 'Just Peachy' (BB SC LB PK/Y, L. Connell, 1986, USA) is a blend of pink and bright yellow. Reclassified from a B size in 1996, it wins easily in both sizes. Easy to grow on a mid-sized plant with many blooms. Wins its Class, Best Semi-Cactus in Show, Best Bloom in Show, Cream of the Crop, and Fabulous Fifty.
McClaren

350 'Victoria Ann' (BB SC LB W/L, Swan Island Dahlias, 2003, USA) is a clean white blending to solid lavender on the margins of the bloom with all petals outlined in lavender. It grows on a very tall healthy plant with many blooms on strong straight stems, making it a valuable cut and show flower.
Swan Island Dahlias

352 'CG Sparkle' (BB SC FL, Larkin/Zydner, 2002, USA) is a brilliant blend of bright yellow and red with excellent petal form and full petalage. It is a easy to grow on a tall healthy plant with many long-stemmed flowers. Wins its Class, Best BB Semi-Cactus, Best Triple BB, and Cream of the Crop.
Alan Fisher

353 'Bold Accent' (BB SC DB L/W, Swan Island Dahlias, 1998, USA) is pure white blending to dark lavender with incurved petals. It grows on a healthy plant with many blooms on strong straight stems. Excellent cut flower for bouquets, floral designs, and baskets.
Swan Island Dahlias

353 'G W's Sun Fire' (BB SC DB PR/Y, Wolfe, 1999*, USA) is yellow blending to tips of purple with excellent petal form and full petalage. It grows on a healthy plant with many early blooms. An attractive cut flower. Wins its Class. S. McClaren

353 'Lois M' (BB SC DB Y/R, McClaren, 1991, USA) is bright yellow at the base of the petal blending to a brilliant red-orange with full petalage. It is easy to grow with many early blooms. Wins its Class and Best BB in Show. Stock is difficult to find. ADS slide library

354 'Hy Pimento' (BB SC V Y/R, W. Holland, 2000, Canada) is pale yellow with dainty red markings and full peta-lage recurving to the stem. It is easy to grow in all climates with strong straight stems. Wins its Class, Best BB Variegated in Show. ADS slide library

355 'Glen Valley Cathy' (BB SC BI Y/R, 1996*), a bicolor of yellow with red tips, has excellent form with full petalage. It grows on a 6 ft. (1.8 m) tall healthy plant with many blooms and produces an abundance of excellent large tubers that keep well in storage. Prefers cool weather with humidity. Jim Rowse

353 'Quiet Riot' (BB SC DB Y/OR/R, D. Jack, 1993*, Canada) is a unique blend of yellow merging with orange and red. Wins its Class on the east coast of North America. Alan Fisher

354 'Poppers' (BB SC V Y/R, Swan Island Dahlias, 2001, USA), a sport of 'Mary Lee McNall', is golden yellow with red variegations and well-formed petals. Makes a great splash of color in the garden but tends to have solid red petals, which can detract from the attrac-tive variegation. Swan Island Dahlias

354 'Hollyhill Candy Stripe' (BB SC V PK/R, T. and M. Kennedy, 2001, USA) is a pastel pink with red markings and full petalage. The notched semi-cactus petals are interspersed with some straight cac-tus forms. Does best in cool weather with humidity. Wins its Class. ADS slide library

355 'Match' (BB SC BI W/PR, Hindrey, 1965, South Africa) has perfect petal form and great petalage. It is easy to grow in all areas on a healthy plant, fully branched, with many early blooms. Wins its Class, Best Semi-Cactus in Show, Best Bicolor in Show, Best BB in Show, Best Bloom in Show, Cream of the Crop, and Fabulous Fifty. S. McClaren

361 'Karras 150' (BB C W, A. Peters, 1996, Australia) is crystal-clear white and of perfect form with full petalage. Many early blooms are carried on a healthy plant with excellent branching and good tuber production. An easy dahlia to grow and show. Wins its Class, Cream of the Crop, and Fabulous Fifty. McClaren

362 'Alpen Marie' (BB IC Y, McClaren, 1992, USA) is lemon-yellow with excellent petal formation. It grows on a healthy plant with good branching and many very early blooms. Wins in a competitive Class. McClaren

362 'Lemon Tart' (BB C Y, Swan Island Dahlias, 1992, USA) is bright yellow with full petalage. It is borne on a healthy low-growing plant that is completely covered with flowers. A valuable border, patio, landscape, and show flower. Wins its Class. Swan Island Dahlias

361 'Prince Charming' (BB C W, Swan Island Dahlias, 2003, USA), a sport of 'Park Princess', is a clean white. It grows on a short healthy plant, making it excellent for borders, landscapes, and containers. Swan Island Dahlias

362 'Colorado Moonshine' (BB IC Y, C. Cook, 2002, USA) is clean yellow with full petalage. It is easy to grow on a healthy plant with straight stems. Wins in a competitive Class and Best BB Cactus in Show. ADS slide library

362 'Superfine' (BB C Y, Geerlings, 1994, Holland) is a clean pastel yellow with perfect petal form and full petalage. Does best in high humidity and cool weather. Wins its Class. Alan Fisher

364 'Curly Que' (BB IC PK, Swan Island Dahlias, 1992, USA) is soft pink with swirling incurved petals. A popular dahlia in the garden and on the show bench, and ideal for artistic arrangements. Prefers cool humid climates. Wins its Class. Swan Island Dahlias

364 'My Robynn' (BB IC PK, Bishop, 2001, USA) is salmon-pink with outstanding form and full petalage. Wins its Class and Cream of the Crop. Alan Fisher

365 'CG Coral' (BB C DP, Larkin/ Zydner, 2001, USA) is dark coral-pink with full petalage and excellent formation. It is easy to grow on a strong healthy plant with good tuber production. Wins its Class and Cream of the Crop. S. McClaren

366 'Araluen Fire' (BB C R, R. Wilkes, 1987, Australia) is bright red with tiny light-colored tips and good petal form. It is easy to grow, a floriferous plant with good tuber production. Does well in all climates and tolerates heat. Wins in a competitive Class. S. McClaren

366 'Redd Devil' (BB C R, Swan Island Dahlias, 1996, USA) is bright red with excellent petal form. Many blooms are borne on a healthy plant on great stems. Excellent cut and basket flower. Swan Island Dahlias

367 'Plum Pretty' (BB IC DR, Swan Island Dahlias, 1995, USA), a striking dark red, grows on a mid-sized plant. Wins its Class. Swan Island Dahlias

368 'Rokewood Opal' (BB C L, 1997*) has excellent form with full petalage and grows on a tall healthy floriferous plant. Easy to grow and tolerates heat. Wins its Class and Cream of the Crop. Alan Fisher

369 'Purple Haze' (BB IC PR, Swan Island Dahlias, 1999, USA) is a rich rosy dahlia with a fluorescent sheen on well-formed petals. Many blooms are borne on a healthy plant. Great substance and strong straight stems make it a valuable cut flower. Swan Island Dahlias

370 'Edith Arthur' (BB C LB Y/PK, Goodman, 1974*) is a pastel yellow and pink blend. The form has great depth, and stems are long and straight. Wins in a competitive Class. Dick Ambrose

370 'Rocky Mountain High' (BB IC LB L/W, C. Cook, 2001, USA) is a blend of white with deep lavender tips on twisted petals. Wins in a very competitive Class. S. McClaren

369 'Skipley Ida' (BB IC PR, R. Williams, 2003, USA) is pale lavender-purple with full petalage. It is easy to grow on a tall healthy plant with many blooms on tall straight stems. A valuable cut and show flower. Wins its Class. ADS slide library

370 'Lilac Mist' (BB IC LB W/L, Swan Island Dahlias, 1985, USA) is white blending to delicate lilac-lavender on the tips. It grows on a tall healthy plant with strong stems. Most attractive in late summer when the weather cools. Swan Island Dahlias

370 'Taratahi Lilac' (BB IC LB L/W, E. and J. Frater, 1996*, New Zealand). Stanley Johnson Award. This is a perfect plant, well branched, and grows in all climates. Every flower on it is the same size, shape, and color, and of great substance, with perfect cut flower stems. Wins its very competitive Class, Best BB Incurved Cactus in Show, Best BB in Show, Best Bloom in Show, Cream of the Crop, and Fabulous Fifty. McClaren

372 'My Fritz' (BB IC FL, Russell, 1980, USA) is a flame of bright red blending to yellow with twisted petals. It grows on a tall healthy plant with many blooms and has good tuber production. Easy to grow, tolerates heat. Wins its Class and Cream of the Crop. McClaren

374 'Alpen Michael T' (BB C V Y/R, McClaren, 2004, USA) is pale yellow with evenly spaced red markings and well-formed petals with full petalage. It is easy to grow on a healthy plant with many early blooms on strong straight stems. Requires cool weather for perfect form. Wins its Class and Best Single and Triple BB Cactus in Show. McClaren

374 'Grandma Jackie' (BB C V Y/DR, Masurat, 1999, USA) is ivory with evenly spaced dark red markings, notched petals, and full petalage. Blooms are borne on strong straight stems. Requires shade for best color. Wins in a competitive Class. Alan Fisher

375 'Jessica' (BB IC BI Y/R, Hale, 1988, USA). Stanley Johnson Award. This is an outstanding show dahlia, with perfect form and excellent color, a striking yellow with brilliant red tips. The blooms are on long straight stems and grow on a tall healthy plant. Wins its Class, Best BB in Show, Best Bicolor in Show, Best Bloom in Show, Cream of the Crop, and Fabulous Fifty. Ben Bartel

375 'Purple Mist' (BB C BI PR/W, Willoughby, 1996, Canada) is well named: its white tips give the effect of a flower covered with mist. It is easy to grow on a healthy plant with excellent tuber production. Does well in cool weather with humidity. Wins in a very difficult Class and Cream of the Crop. S. McClaren

381 'Janken Jubilee' (BB LC W, Minor, 1997, USA) is white with full petalage. It grows on a healthy plant with blooms on straight stems. Prefers cool weather with high humidity. Alan Fisher

382 'Hissy Fitz' (BB LC Y, Swan Island Dahlias, 1999, USA) is bright yellow with well-formed petals and full petalage. It has great substance with a long shelf life—valuable as a cut, arranging, basket, and show flower. Wins its Class, Best BB Laciniated in Show, Best BB in Show, Best Bloom in Show, and Cream of the Crop. Swan Island Dahlias

384 'Coral Frills' (BB LC PK, Swan Island Dahlias, 1991, USA) has pink blends with notched petals and a creamy yellow center. Easy to grow on a healthy plant whose many laterals produce an abundance of early blooms. Strong straight stems—a cut, garden, and show flower. Wins its Class. Swan Island Dahlias

385 'Snoho Penny' (BB LC DP, Bonneywell, 1997, USA) is dark pink with well-formed petals and full petalage. It grows on a lacy-leaved plant and likes cool climate and high humidity. Wins its Class and Best BB Laciniated in Show. ADS slide library

386 'Caproz Angelika' (BB LC R, Probizanski, 1998, USA) is purplish red with good form and full petalage. An easy dahlia to grow on a healthy plant with good flower production. Its color makes it an attractive cut flower. Wins its Class. McClaren

388 'Spenser's Angel' (BB LC L, Clack, 1998, USA) has excellent petals with full petalage. It grows on a healthy plant with many blooms and shows well on the west coast of Canada and the United States. S. McClaren

389 'Valley Prince' (BB LC PR, Peterson, 1974, USA), a purple with excellent form and full petalage, was reclassified from a miniature to a BB in 1989 and in 1997 to a laciniated. Many blooms are carried on a tall well-branched plant. Easy to grow and good tuber production. Wins its Class and Cream of the Crop. McClaren

390 'Alpen Fern' (BB LC LB Y/PK, McClaren, 1983, USA), a blend of pastel yellow and pink with full petalage, was reclassified in 1995 from an informal decorative. It grows on a strong healthy plant with many early blooms with great stems. Good substance makes it an attractive cut flower. Wins in a very competitive Class. McClaren

390 'Marlene Joy' (BB LC LB W/PK, Steenfott, 1989*, USA) is clean white blending to pink at the tips, with well-formed petals and full petalage. It is easy to grow with many blooms. A great show flower, it was introduced as a B cactus (laciniated), reclassified as a B laciniated in 1993, and changed again to BB laciniated in 2002. Wins its Class, Best B and BB Laciniated in Show, Best B and BB in Show, Cream of the Crop, and Fabulous Fifty. Ben Bartel

390 'My Beverly' (BB LC LB DP/Y, Simmons, 1999, USA), a blend of bright yellow with pastel dark-pink tips, has outstanding form and full petalage. Wins in a very competitive Class, Best Laciniated BB in Show, Best BB in Show, Cream of the Crop, and Fabulous Fifty. Alan Fisher

392 'Cheyenne' (BB LC FL, Buddin, 1975, USA) is a brilliant red with a touch of yellow, with excellent petals and full petalage. It is a healthy plant with strong stems and grows in all climates. Wins its Class and Cream of the Crop. Dick Ambrose

391 'Kaiwera Gold' (BB LC BR, McNoe, 1978, New Zealand), a pale yellow-bronze, was reclassified from a semi-cactus in 1994. Wins its Class and Cream of the Crop. McClaren

CHAPTER 5

Miniature and Waterlily

MINIATURE

When the ADS began classifying dahlias by size, all flowers under 4 in. (10 cm) were miniatures; included were forms such as single, peony, collarette, and anemone, which dahlias have since been separately classified. The miniature in the present ADS classification is under 4 in. (10 cm) and takes the following forms: formal decorative, informal decorative, semi-cactus, straight cactus, incurved cactus, and laciniated.

Aptly named, the miniature dahlia has small ray florets, and the flower is diminutive in size. From the earliest size classification of dahlias, it has always been called miniature.

The photos in this section of the chapter represent the 15 color classes and include examples of the formal decorative, informal decorative, semi-cactus, straight cactus, and laciniated forms.

MINIATURE PHOTOS

401 'Mary Hammett' (M FD W, K. Hammett, 1991, New Zealand) is a clean clear white, often with a blush of lavender. It has perfect formation with full petalage and grows on a healthy plant with many blooms and excellent tuber production. Does well in all climates and areas of the world but requires cooler weather for a perfect bloom. Wins its Class, Best Miniature in Show, Best Bloom in Show, Cream of the Crop, and Fabulous Fifty. McClaren

402 'Camano Dot' (M FD Y, R. Ambrose, 2002, USA) is clean soft yellow with perfect form and full petalage. It is easy to grow on a healthy plant with many blooms. Wins its Class. S. McClaren

402 'Tonya' (M FD Y, Hilberg, 1989, USA), a clear pastel yellow, grows on a healthy floriferous plant with excellent tuber production. Wins its Class, Best Miniature in Show, Cream of the Crop, and Fabulous Fifty. McClaren

403 'Gingeroo' (M FD OR, Swan Island Dahlias, 1994, USA) is a vibrant nonfading orange with rounded petals. It grows on a healthy plant with an abundance of blooms and firm substance. Wins its Class. Swan Island Dahlias

403 'Oreti Ginger' (M FD OR, W. Jack, New Zealand) is bright orange with petals split at ends and full petalage recurving to the stem. It is easy to grow on a tall healthy plant with many early blooms. Excellent cut flower, with well-proportioned straight stems and good substance. Wins its Class. Walter Jack

403 'Rose Toscano' (M FD OR, H. and B. Brown, 1991, USA). Lynn B. Dudley and Stanley Johnson awards. This orange dahlia is a perfect mid-sized miniature with excellent petal form. Many blooms are carried on a tall healthy plant with full branching; the strong stems are correctly proportioned to the bloom. Excellent tuber production; tubers keep well in storage. An attractive cut flower with great substance and a long shelf life. Wins its Class, Best Single and Triple Miniature in Show, Best Bloom in Show, Cream of the Crop, and Fabulous Fifty. McClaren

403 'Simplicity' (M FD OR, Swan Island Dahlias, 1998, USA) is deep rich apricot-tangerine with a lavender reverse and full petalage. Many blooms are borne on a healthy compact low-growing plant—an excellent patio specimen.
Swan Island Dahlias

404 'Jitterbug' (M FD PK, Swan Island Dahlias, 1995, USA) is salmon-pink with pointed petals. Early small blooms are carried on a low-growing compact bush; flowers are produced into late fall. Wins its Class. Swan Island Dahlias

405 'Rebecca Lynn' (M FD DP, L. Connell, 1987, USA). Lynn B. Dudley and Derrill W. Hart awards. This is a perfect dahlia, dark lavender-pink with full petalage and tightly formed petals. The blooms are petite. Wins its very competitive Class, Best Formal Decorative Miniature, Best Miniature in Show, Best Flower in Show, Cream of the Crop, and Fabulous Fifty. McClaren

404 'Bubblegum' (M FD PK, Swan Island Dahlias, 1996, USA), most aptly named for its color, grows on a tall healthy well-branched plant with many early blooms. The early bloom has a waterlily form but develops into a formal decorative with maturity. Makes a great cut flower. Swan Island Dahlias

404 'Melissa M' (M FD PK, Swan Island Dahlias, 1992, USA) is bright nonfading fuchsia-pink with incurved petals. It grows on a tall healthy plant with blooms on straight stiff stems. Wins its Class. Swan Island Dahlias

406 'Ali Oop' (M FD R, Swan Island Dahlias, 1995, USA) is nonfading red with full petalage. It is easy to grow on a healthy plant with many early blooms.
Swan Island Dahlias

406 'Lollipop' (M FD R, Swan Island Dahlias, 1990, USA) is orange-red with rounded petals and full petalage. Dainty blooms are carried on a short plant, making it ideal for the border and landscape, or as a potted plant. Swan Island Dahlias

406 'Spellbreaker' (M FD R, Swan Island Dahlias, 2000, USA) is raspberry-red with well-formed petals and full petalage. It grows on a compact healthy plant. Valuable as a container plant. Swan Island Dahlias

406 'Woodland's Uptown Girl' (M FD R, Mischler, 1998, USA). Derrill W. Hart Award. This nonfading red has excellent petal form and full petalage. A healthy floriferous plant, it does well in all areas. Wins in a difficult Class, Best Miniature Formal Decorative, Best Miniature in Show, and Cream of the Crop. McClaren

406 'Pazazz' (M FD R, Swan Island Dahlias, 1992, USA) is nonfading bright red with rounded petals. It grows on a compact low-growing floriferous plant. Easy to grow from small tubers. Wins its Class. Swan Island Dahlias

406 'Tui Connie' (M FD R, Buckley, 1996, New Zealand) is nonfading bright red with excellent petal form, full petalage, and strong straight stems. It is easy to grow on a healthy plant with many blooms. Good tuber production. Wins in a competitive Class. McClaren

407 'Alpen Sheen' (M FD DR, McClaren, 1981, USA) is nonfading dark red, nearly black, with a lighter reverse and well-formed petals with full petalage. It is easy to grow on a healthy plant with many early blooms. Wins its Class, Best Miniature Formal Decorative in Show, and Cream of the Crop. ADS slide library

407 'Bing' (M FD DR, Larkin/Zydner, 1997, USA) is nonfading dark red with a lighter reverse. It has excellent petal form and full petalage. Easy to grow on a strong healthy plant with many blooms. Wins in a very competitive Class. ADS slide library

407 'Arabian Night' (M FD DR, Weijers, 1951, Holland) is nonfading dark red, nearly black, with broad flat petal form. It is easy to grow on a strong healthy plant with many tubers that keep well in storage. Does well in all areas of the United States. Reclassified from a formal decorative to a waterlily in 1984 and back to a formal decorative in 1986. Wins in both classes, Best Miniature Formal Decorative, and Cream of the Crop. Global Publishing

407 'Burma Gem' (M FD DR, Swan Island Dahlias, 1991, USA) is a dark red sport of 'Red Garnet' with many of the same growth habits: many early blooms are borne on a tall healthy well-branched plant. The stems are strong and straight, making it an ideal cut flower—shows well too. Wins its Class. Swan Island Dahlias

407 'Barbarry Red Baron' (M FD DR, Davies, 2002, UK). Lynn B. Dudley Award. This nonfading dark red with tightly rolled petals and full petalage is easy to grow in all areas of the United States with many perfect blooms. Wins its very competitive Class, Best Miniature Formal Decorative in Show, Best Miniature in Show, Cream of the Crop, and Fabulous Fifty. ADS slide library

407 'Fidalgo Blacky' (M FD DR, Matthies, 1993, USA) is appropriately named: this small bloom is nearly black, a nonfading dark red with excellent cupped petals and full petalage. Perfect for an artistic arrangement that needs black. Wins in a very competitive Class.
McClaren

408 'Derek Sean' (M FD L, Swan Island Dahlias, 1990, USA) is light lavender with an attractive sheen. It grows on a tall fully branched plant with many early blooms. Easy to disbud, making it a good cut flower. Wins its Class.
Swan Island Dahlias

409 'Bit O' Bret' (M FD PR, R. Ambrose, 1981, USA) is dark, nearly black, with well-formed pointed petals and full petalage. It is easy to grow on a strong healthy plant with many blooms. Wins its Class, Best Miniature Formal Decorative, and Best Miniature in Show.
ADS slide library

407 'Red Garnet' (M FD DR, Swan Island Dahlias, 1967, USA), a velvety dark red with pointed petals, grows on a tall well-branched plant with many blooms. Wins its Class.
Swan Island Dahlias

408 'Tiny Dancer' (M FD L, Swan Island Dahlias, 1995, USA), a deep lavender with rounded petals, grows on a compact floriferous plant. A good cut flower.
Swan Island Dahlias

409 'Gonzo Grape' (M FD PR, Swan Island Dahlias, 2000, USA) is deep fuchsia-purple with rounded petals and full petalage. It is easy to grow on a healthy plant with many blooms on tall stiff stems, making it a valuable cut and show flower. Wins its Class and Best Single and Triple Miniature in Show.
Swan Island Dahlias

409 'Oreti Liz' (M FD PR, W. Jack, 2001, New Zealand) is a perfect lavender-purple flower. It is easy to grow on a strong healthy plant with good tuber production. Wins in a very competitive Class. Strong stems and great substance make it a fine cut flower. Walter Jack

409 'SB's Becky' (M FD PR, Boley, 2002*, USA) is blends of dark purple with pleated petals, perfect for the form, and full petalage recurving to the stem. It is an easy dahlia to grow on a healthy plant with many blooms. Wins its Class and Best Miniature Formal Decorative in Show. ADS slide library

410 'Be-Bop' (M FD LB Y/PK, Swan Island Dahlias, 1996, USA) is pastel yellow blending to a soft pink with round petals. It flowers profusely and early on a healthy low-growing plant, making it useful for borders. Swan Island Dahlias

409 'Patty Jo' (M FD PR, Kutschara, 1983, USA) is reddish purple with full petalage. It is easy to grow on a tall healthy plant with many blooms. Wins its Class and Best Miniature Formal Decorative in Show. ADS slide library

409 'Thelma's Delight' (M FD PR, T. Johnson, 1981, USA) is reddish purple with pointed petals. It grows on a healthy plant with many early blooms. Wins its Class and Best Miniature Formal Decorative in Show. ADS slide library

410 'Dear Heart' (M FD LB W/DP, Olson, 1983, USA) is an unusual shade of dark pink in the center blending to deep pink and white in the margins with well-formed petals and full petalage. An attractive garden and cut flower. ADS slide library

410 'French Doll' (M FD LB Y/PK, Swan Island Dahlias, 1999, USA) is soft salmon-apricot blending to pastel yellow in the center with rounded petals and full petalage. It grows on a healthy plant with great stems for cutting.
Swan Island Dahlias

410 'Morning Dew' (M FD LB Y/L, Stowell, 1966, USA) is pale yellow blending to lavender. Formerly classified as a waterlily but with too many petals, hence the reclassification. The petals are flat but lack the petalage needed to recurve to the stem. It is easy to grow on a healthy plant with many blooms on strong stems. Valuable as a cut, garden, and show flower. Wins in a competitive Class. McClaren

410 'Peek A Boo' (M FD LB W/L, Swan Island Dahlias, 1999, USA) is lavender-pink blending to white. It grows on a healthy plant with many blooms. A long shelf life and straight stems with firm substance make it a great cut flower.
Swan Island Dahlias

410 'Last Dance' (M FD LB L/W, Swan Island Dahlias, 1994, USA) is a very pale lavender, nearly white, blending to a darker lavender center. It grows on a healthy plant with many blooms and is easy to grow, with good tuber production. An attractive cut flower. Wins in a competitive Class. Swan Island Dahlias

410 'Peaches-N-Cream' (M FD LB OR/W, Blue Dahlia Garden, 1993, USA). Lynn B. Dudley Award. This pumpkin-orange blending to large light tips is easy to grow on a healthy plant with many blooms. Tolerates heat. Wins its Class, Best Formal Decorative in Show, Best Bloom in Show, Cream of the Crop, and Fabulous Fifty. S. McClaren

411 'G W's Sunshine' (M FD BR, Wolfe, 2001, USA) is light bronze with excellent petal form and full petalage. It grows on a healthy fully branched plant with many small blooms. Strong straight stems and firm substance make it a desirable cut flower. Tolerates heat. Wins its Class and Best Single and Triple Miniature in Show. McClaren

411 'Jabberbox' (M FD BR, Swan Island Dahlias, 1995, USA) is blends of yellowish bronze. The low-growing plant blooms all season. Wins its Class.
Swan Island Dahlias

413 'Bristol Dandy' (M FD DB DR/Y, Franklin, 2001, USA) is golden yellow with a blush of dark red, giving it a bronze appearance. It has pleated full petalage of firm substance and makes a long-lasting cut flower. Wins in a very competitive Class. McClaren

413 'Daniel Edward' (M FD DB W/PR, Swan Island Dahlias, 1989, USA) is white blending to a deep purple with a dark purple center. It grows on a healthy plant with many blooms on strong straight stems. A great cut flower. Wins its Class.
Swan Island Dahlias

412 'Mardy Gras' (M FD FL, Swan Island Dahlias, 1999, USA) is bright orange blending to brilliant yellow on each pointed petal. Small blooms are carried on a healthy plant. Great stems and good substance make it an excellent cut flower. Swan Island Dahlias

413 'Carrie' (M FD DB W/PR, McClaren, 1982, USA) is a blend of white and purple with small white tips. Many small blooms with tightly pointed petals and full petalage are carried on a tall healthy fully branched plant. Tubers store well. An excellent seed parent and a long-lasting cut flower of firm substance. Wins in a competitive Class. McClaren

413 'Foxy Lady' (M FD DB DP/Y, Swan Island Dahlias, 1994, USA) is dusty rose blending to ivory with a deep rose reverse. It is borne on straight stems. Wins its Class. Swan Island Dahlias

413 'Raz-Ma-Taz' (M FD DB Y/R, Swan Island Dahlias, 1993, USA) is a dark blend, red predominant and touches of bright yellow in the center, with excellent petal formation. It is easy to grow with many dainty flowers. Eye-catching on the show table and as a cut flower. Wins its Class. Swan Island Dahlias

414 'Alpen Jewel' (M FD V PR/R, McClaren, 1991, USA) is a variegated light purple with red markings. It is easy to grow with many early small blooms. Excellent seed parent. Wins its Class, Best Variegated Miniature in Show, and Cream of the Crop. McClaren

415 'Brandon James' (M FD BI Y/W, Swan Island Dahlias, 1994, USA) is golden yellow, a color not often seen in bicolors, with well-marked tips of white. It grows on a tall healthy plant that blooms early and continues to flower abundantly throughout the season. Works well as a cut flower in bouquets and artistic designs. Swan Island Dahlias

413 'Ted's Choice' (M FD DB L/PR, Swan Island Dahlias, 1989, USA) is blends of lavender and purple with a purple reverse. It grows on a healthy plant with many blooms on straight stems. Originally classified as a BB but reclassified in 1999 to a miniature; in many areas it still grows as a BB. Wins its Class and Best Formal Decorative in Show. Swan Island Dahlias

415 'B-Man' (M FD BI PR/W, Swan Island Dahlias, 1998,USA) is a bicolor of deep purple with white tips, which tend to be uneven. It is easy to grow on a healthy plant and makes a great splash of color in the garden. Excellent cut flower with great stems. Swan Island Dahlias

415 'Checkers' (M FD BI DR/W, Swan Island Dahlias, 2001, USA) is a perfectly consistent bicolor of dark red evenly tipped in white with excellent petal form and full petalage. It is easy to grow on a mid-sized plant that has lush lacy foliage. Lights up the garden and makes an attractive cut flower. Wins its Class, Best Miniature Bicolor in Show, and Best Basket in Show. Swan Island Dahlias

415 'Fuzzy Wuzzy' (M FD BI PK/W, Swan Island Dahlias, 2000, USA) is bright pink with white tips on the pleated notched petals. It is easy to grow on a strong healthy plant with blooms on sturdy stems. Wins its Class and Best Single and Triple Miniature in Show. Swan Island Dahlias

422 'Moonstruck' (M ID Y, Swan Island Dahlias, 1996, USA) is pastel cream-yellow with well-formed petals. Many early blooms are carried on great stems on a low-growing plant. Wins its Class, Best Single and Triple Miniature Informal Decorative in Show, and Best Miniature in Show. Swan Island Dahlias

421 'Hockley Nymph' (M ID W, Spencer, 1953, UK) is a clean ivory. It is easy to grow on a healthy plant with many early blooms on strong straight stems. Valuable cut and show flower. Wins its Class, Best Informal Decorative in Show, and Cream of the Crop. McClaren

426 'Ruby Red' (M ID R, L. Connell, 1987, USA), a sharp brilliant red, is so lacking in petals it approaches a miniature waterlily in form. It is an easy flower to grow with many blooms—a great small cut flower. Wins its Class and Best Miniature Informal Decorative in Show. Ben Bartel

429 'Hamilton Midnight' (M ID PR, Hamilton, 1999, Canada) is a purple dahlia with a light reverse and full petalage. It is easy to grow on a healthy plant with many early blooms. Attractive in collections and baskets. Wins its Class and Best Miniature Informal Decorative. Ben Bartel

430 'Prom Queen' (M ID LB W/L, Heines, 1990, USA). Derrill W. Hart Award. This miniature is a blend of white to pastel lavender with pastel lavender lining each petal's edge. It grows well in all areas of North America on a tall healthy plant with great branching and many blooms. Tolerates heat. Classified as a formal decorative from 1995 to 1997. Wins both classes, Best Miniature Informal Decorative, Cream of the Crop, and Fabulous Fifty. McClaren

442 'Bristol Sunny' (M SC Y, Franklin, 2000, USA) is bright clear yellow with outstanding petal form and full petalage. It is easy to grow in all areas of the United States, producing many blooms on a healthy plant. An exceptional show flower. Wins its Class and Cream of the Crop. McClaren

444 'Mary Jo' (M SC PK, Franz, 1968, USA). Stanley Johnson Award. The perfect miniature, this dahlia is a pinkish blend of pastel yellow and orange with great petal form and full petalage. It is easy to grow on a healthy mid-sized plant; all blooms are the same size, shape, and color, making it easy to show in multiple classes. Grows and shows particularly well in the western United States. Wins its Class, Best Single and Triple Miniature in Show, Cream of the Crop, and Fabulous Fifty. McClaren

433 'Jacy' (M ID DB W/DP, McClaren, 1980, USA) is a blend of white to dark pink with an edging of dark pink on each petal. Easy to grow in all areas, it blooms early and profusely and produces an abundance of tubers. Tolerates heat. Wins its Class. McClaren

444 'Heather Marie' (M SC PK, Swan Island Dahlias, 1983, USA) is a soft salmon-pink with incurved petals. It grows from small tubers on a healthy plant with many blooms. Sturdy stems make it a good cut and show flower. Wins its Class. Swan Island Dahlias

446 'Alpen Gem' (M SC R, McClaren, 1981, USA) is bright red and easy to grow on strong healthy plants. The many tubers produced keep well in storage. Resistant to spider mites. Wins its Class, Best Miniature Semi-Cactus in Show, Best Miniature in Show, and Cream of the Crop. ADS slide library

446 'Mathew Alan' (M SC R, Swan Island Dahlias, 2003, USA) is rich red with the reverse a dark red. Compact healthy plants produce many cut flowers. Swan Island Dahlias

449 'Deliah' (M SC PR, L. Connell, 1998*, USA) is reddish purple with excellent form and full petalage. It is easy to grow in all areas of North America, tolerates heat, and has great stems. Wins its Class and Cream of the Crop. Alan Fisher

450 'Coral Baby' (M SC LB PK/Y, Swan Island Dahlias, 1999, USA) is coral-pink blending to pastel yellow in the center, an in-demand color combination for cut flowers. It has full petalage and grows on a tall well-branched plant with many blooms and strong straight stems. The blooms have a long shelf life. Swan Island Dahlias

453 'Wildcat' (M SC DB DR/Y, Swan Island Dahlias, 1998, USA) is brilliant dark red blending to a bright yellow with full petalage. It grows on a tall healthy plant with many blooms on strong straight stems. A good cut and show flower. Wins its Class, Best Miniature Semi-Cactus in Show, and Best Miniature in Show. Swan Island Dahlias

455 'Alpen Joy' (M SC BI W/PR, McClaren, 1993, USA) is a bicolor of white with purple tips. It is easy to grow on a tall well-branched healthy plant with excellent stems. Firm substance makes it a great cut flower. Does well in all areas of North America and tolerates heat. Wins its Class. McClaren

461 'Alpen Snowflake' (M C W, McClaren, 1991, USA) is clean white with perfect form and full petalage. It is easy to grow on a well-branched healthy plant with many blooms and abundant tuber production. Does well in all areas of North America. Tolerates heat. An excellent seed parent. Wins its Class, Best Single and Triple Miniature Cactus in Show, Best Miniature in Show, Best Bloom in Show, Cream of the Crop, and Fabulous Fifty. McClaren

462 'Kathy's Choice' (M C Y, Canning, 1999, USA). Lynn B. Dudley and Stanley Johnson awards. This perfect miniature cactus has won every award offered by the ADS. Lemon-yellow with full petalage, it is easy to grow with many perfect blooms, all the same size, shape, and form. It grows on a well-branched plant, and the tubers keep well in storage. Does well in all areas of North America. Wins its Class, Best Miniature Cactus in Show, Best Single and Multiple Miniature in Show, Best Cactus in Show, Best Bloom in Show, Best Triple in Show, Best Multiple Blooms in Show, Best Exhibit in Show, Cream of the Crop, and Fabulous Fifty. S. McClaren

465 'Monkstown Diane' (M C DP, 1995) is blends of dark pink with mature petals of cactus form and full petalage; many of the ray florets are notched. A useful cut and show flower. Wins its Class.
Alan Fisher

465 'Park Princess' (M C DP, Maarse, 1959, Holland) is a soft dark pink. Reclassified from a BB in 2003, it is easy to grow in all areas on a healthy low-growing plant with many early blooms—a great border flower throughout the season. Produces an abundance of tubers that keep in long storage. Often seen in parks and dahlia gardens, where many blooms are massed for display. Wins its Class. Global Publishing

464 'Oreti Melody' (M C PK, W. Jack, New Zealand) is pink with pointed tips, perfect petal form, and full petalage. It is easy to grow on a healthy plant with many blooms. Wins its Class. Walter Jack

466 'Alpen Rhicky' (M C R, McClaren, 1992, USA) is brilliant red with well-formed petals and full petalage. It is easy to grow on a healthy plant with many early blooms. The tubers are abundant and keep in long storage. Wins its Class, Best Miniature Single and Triple Cactus in Show, and Cream of the Crop.
McClaren

469 'Alpen Treasure' (M C PR, McClaren, 1997, USA) is a rich fuchsia with perfect form. It is easy to grow on a healthy plant with many early blooms. Excellent tuber production. Strong stems and firm substance make it useful for cut flowers and artistic designs. Wins its Class and Cream of the Crop. McClaren

470 'Alpen Twinkle' (M C LB W/PR, McClaren, 1991, USA), a blend of white with pastel lavender-purple petals, has excellent form with blunt petals and full petalage. It is easy to grow on a mid-sized plant with many early blooms. Wins in a competitive Class. McClaren

470 'Glenbank Twinkle' (M C LB W/PR, Davidson, 1982*, Australia). Stanley Johnson Award. One of the best miniature cactus dahlias, this outstanding white blending with dark purple has perfect form with full petalage. Does well in all areas and tolerates heat. Wins its Class, Best Miniature Cactus in Show, Best Miniature in Show, Best Cactus in Show, Best Bloom in Show, Best Triple in Show, Cream of the Crop, and Fabulous Fifty. Alan Fisher

472 'Fall Fiesta' (M C FL Y/OR, Swan Island Dahlias, 2003, USA) is yellow blending to bright orange with well-formed petals. It grows on a tall healthy plant with many blooms on sturdy stems, making it a valuable cut and show flower. Swan Island Dahlias

472 'Weston Spanish Dancer' (M C FL R/Y, McLelland, 2000*, UK) is an outstanding flame of yellow blending to brilliant red petals. It has an exceptional form with great full petalage—a perfect miniature cactus. Easy to grow on a healthy plant with many early blooms. Wins its Class, Best Miniature Cactus in Show, Best Single and Triple Miniature in Show, Best Cactus in Show, Best Bloom in Show, Cream of the Crop, and Fabulous Fifty. McClaren

473 'Light Touch' (M C DB PR/W, Almand, 1994, USA), a blend of white with dark purple tips, offers excellent form and full petalage on an easy-to-grow floriferous plant. Wins in a very competitive Class. S. McClaren

474 'Shea's Rainbow' (M C V PK/Y, Clack, 1999, USA), an interesting variegation of yellow with pink markings, has excellent form and full petalage. It grows and shows well in the cool weather and high humidity of the west coast of North America. Wins its Class, Best Miniature Variegated Bloom in Show, Best Miniature, Cream of the Crop, and Fabulous Fifty. S. McClaren

475 'Alpen Jean' (M C BI PR/W, McClaren, 1996, USA), a bicolor with white petals and dark purple tips, has excellent form and full petalage. It is easy to grow on a healthy plant with mid to late blooms. Prefers cool weather and humidity. Wins its Class. McClaren

483 'Alfa Max' (M LC OR, M. Camotes, 2001*, USA), an early orange, is easy to grow on a healthy floriferous plant with good tuber production. Wins its Class. McClaren

WATERLILY

Special characteristics make the waterlily unique among dahlias: the outer ray florets are broad and slightly cupped with rounded tips; the flower depth is shallow.

Among the earliest named dahlia forms, the waterlily was recognized as early as 1826. The waterlily has been called many names, camellia-flowered, nymphaea (Latin for "waterlily"), and nymphea (corruption of same) among them. The early waterlilies were included with the double forms, and for a time they were a subclass of formal decorative. Waterlilies were first recognized by the ADS in 1964 (Weland 1997b). The ADS originally classified the waterlily (first rendered as two words, water lily) as a B and then reclassified it as a BB; in 1977 it was listed as a separate form.

The waterlily's popularity has waxed and waned over the years, as the recurved petals of the double dahlias likewise became more, or less, attractive to growers than the flat saucer-shaped waterlily petals. Recently the waterlily has become tremendously popular and much in demand as a cut flower for floral designs. The photos in this section of the chapter represent 14 color classes.

WATERLILY PHOTOS

601 'Angel's Dust' (WL W, Swan Island Dahlias, 1997, USA). Derrill W. Hart Award. This clean white dahlia with a pale lavender blush grows on a tall healthy heavily branched plant with many blooms. The stems are excellent, making it a perfect cut flower. Wins in a very competitive Class.
Swan Island Dahlias

601 'Swan Lake' (WL W, Swan Island Dahlias, 1998, USA) tends to be too deep for an ideal waterlily, but it is a small bloom, well suited for borders and containers. Swan Island Dahlias

602 'Leo Jelito' (WL Y, 1999*) is bright clean yellow with perfect petals and ideal form, easy to grow on a healthy plant with excellent stems. It is a great cut and show flower. Wins its Class and Best Single and Triple Waterlily in Show.
Alan Fisher

603 'Camano Marmalade' (WL OR, R. Ambrose, 1995*, USA) is soft orange with well-formed cupped petals. Strong stems make it a valuable cut flower. Wins its Class. S. McClaren

603 'Pam Howden' (WL OR, 1997*) is orange with light orange blends; the form of the bloom is perfect. It is easy to grow on a healthy fully branched plant and produces an abundance of tubers that keep well in storage. Excellent seed parent. Wins its Class, Best Single and Triple Waterlily in Show, Cream of the Crop, and Fabulous Fifty. McClaren

604 'Coral Beauty' (WL PK, 1991*) is coral-pink. It is easy to grow on a healthy plant with many blooms on strong stems. Useful as a cut and show flower. Wins in a competitive Class. McClaren

604 'Gerrie Hoek' (WL PK, Hoek, 1942, Holland), a pink with perfect petal form, is often used as the ideal waterlily. It is easy to grow on a healthy plant with excellent tuber production; the tubers keep well in storage. Valuable as a cut, garden, and show flower. Wins in a very competitive Class, Best Single and Triple Waterlily in Show, and Cream of the Crop. McClaren

604 'Yvonne' (WL PK, Geerlings, 1991, Holland). The dahlia world has been blessed with many outstanding waterlilies from Holland, including this rose-pink blending to a lighter pink. It has great substance and stems—a perfect cut flower—and is easy to grow on a healthy fully branched plant. Tolerates heat. Wins in a very competitive Class and Best Waterlily in Show. McClaren

606 'My Valentine' (WL R, Geisert, 1986, USA) is a brilliant nonfading red on strong straight stems, making it a perfect cut flower. It is easy to grow on a healthy fully branched plant with many large 5 in. (12.5 cm) blooms. Wins its Class. McClaren

604 'Patty Cake' (WL PK, Swan Island Dahlias, 1998, USA) is a soft delicate pink blending to a pastel pink toward the margin of the bloom; petals show some notching during hot weather. It grows on a healthy well-branched plant with an abundance of blooms. The color makes it a valuable cut flower. Swan Island Dahlias

605 'Wildwood Marie' (WL DP, Papierski, 1993, USA). Lynn B. Dudley Award. This dahlia, a dark pink blending to pale yellow, has excellent cupped petals with a perfect center and well-shaped form. Easy to grow, it blooms in mid season on a healthy fully branched plant and produces many perfect tubers that have a long storage life. Wins its Class, Best Waterlily in Show, Cream of the Crop, and Fabulous Fifty. S. McClaren

606 'Red Velvet' (WL R, Tickner, 1963, Australia) is a brilliant nonfading red with perfect cupped petals and ideal form. It is easy to grow in all areas with many early blooms. Wins its Class, Best Single and Triple Waterlily in Show, Best Bloom in Show, Cream of the Crop, and Fabulous Fifty. S. McClaren

606 'Taratahi Ruby' (WL R, E. and J. Frater, 1997*, New Zealand) offers large 5 in. (12.5 cm) bright nonfading red blooms on strong straight stems early in the season. It is easy to grow on a tall healthy floriferous plant with excellent tuber production; tubers keep well in storage. A great show and perfect cut flower, and an excellent seed parent. Wins its Class, Best Single and Triple Waterlily in Show, Best Bloom in Show, Cream of the Crop, and Fabulous Fifty. McClaren

608 'Lauren Michele' (WL L, Swan Island Dahlias, 1990, USA) is a petite 3 in. (7.5 cm) lavender bloom with a reverse of purple. It is easy to grow on a healthy fully branched plant. Perfect for artistic designs, bouquets, and cut flowers. Wins its Class and Cream of the Crop. Swan Island Dahlias

608 'Sandia Shomei' (WL L, Boley, 2001, USA) is clean pastel lavender with perfectly formed petals. It is easy to grow on a healthy plant. A cut and show flower of firm substance. Wins its Class, Best Single and Triple Waterlily in Show. ADS slide library

608 'Brushstrokes' (WL L, Swan Island Dahlias, 1996, USA) is lavender with painterly undertones of rose and well-formed cupped petals. Large 5 in. (12.5 cm) blooms are carried early in the season on a healthy 5 ft. (1.5 m) fully branched plant. Strong sturdy stems, a perfect cut flower. Wins its Class, Best Waterlily in Show, and Cream of the Crop. Swan Island Dahlias

608 'Randi Dawn' (WL L, Swan Island Dahlias, 1985, USA), a blend of soft lavenders, is possibly too deep for an ideal waterlily but makes an ideal cut flower. Large blooms are borne on a tall sturdy healthy plant. Swan Island Dahlias

609 'Skipley Fair Lady' (WL PR, R. Williams, 1993, USA). Derrill W. Hart Award. This dahlia, an unusual arrangement of blends of purple, is easy to grow on a healthy plant with many blooms on strong straight stems. A valuable garden and cut flower. McClaren

610 'Bea Paradise' (WL LB W/L, Paradise, 2003, USA), a white blending to lavender, has excellent form and perfect cupped petals. It is easy to grow on a healthy plant with many early blooms with long straight stems. Excellent cut and show flower. Wins its Class, Best Single and Triple Waterlily, and Cream of the Crop. Alan Fisher

610 'Bitsy' (WL LB W/L, Swan Island Dahlias, 2000, USA), a sport of 'China Doll', is a blend of white and dark lavender. Many early long-lasting blooms are borne on a healthy low-growing plant. Excellent for landscape borders, valuable for limited spaces and as a potted plant. Swan Island Dahlias

610 'Bracken Ballerina' (WL LB PK/W, Nauman, 1986*, Australia), a blend of pale pink and white with perfect cupped petals and excellent form, was reclassified from a pink to a light blend in 1996. It grows on a healthy fully branched plant with many early blooms. Strong straight stems and firm substance make it a perfect cut flower. A good seed parent. Wins in a very competitive Class. S. McClaren

610 'Bracken Triune' (WL LB BR/Y, Nauman, 1992*, Australia) is bronze blending to yellow. It is easy to grow on a healthy plant with blooms on straight stems. A valuable cut and show flower. Wins its Class. McClaren

610 'China Doll' (WL LB Y/PK, Swan Island Dahlias, 1994, USA), a light yellow blending to a soft pink, blooms profusely throughout the season on a healthy low-growing plant. Long-lasting as a cut flower, and an attractive border plant for landscaping. Wins in a very competitive Class. Swan Island Dahlias

610 'Juul's Lotus' (WL LB L/W, Juul, 1998, USA). Derrill W. Hart Award. This waterlily, a white blending to soft lavender, was classified as white prior to 2003. It is easy to grow on a healthy fully branched plant with many blooms. Does well in a cool climate, with high humidity and shade. Wins its Class, Best Waterlily in Show, Best Bloom in Show, Cream of the Crop, and Fabulous Fifty. S. McClaren

610 'Kyoh-Komachi' (WL LB Y/L, Konishi, 1992*, Japan) is a bright yellow blending to lavender with true waterlily form. It grows on a mid-sized plant with many early blooms. Easy to grow with good tuber production. Wins its Class. Yusaku Konishi

610 'Miss Molly' (WL LB PK/Y, Swan Island Dahlias, 2003, USA) is bright yellow blending to salmon-pink on the outer tips. It grows on a healthy plant that produces small blooms of good substance and with strong stems—a valuable cut flower. Swan Island Dahlias

610 'Nepos' (WL LB W/L, Lombaert, 1958, Belgium) is a pleasing white blended to pale lavender with perfect cupped petals with excellent form. Among the oldest waterlilies being grown and shown, and formerly a BB formal decorative, it was reclassified as a waterlily in 1974. The small 3.5 in. (8.75 cm) blooms are easy to grow on a healthy plant; the many tubers produced have a long storage life. Does well in all areas and tolerates heat. A good seed parent. Makes an excellent show flower as a single or multiple blooms. Wins its Class, Best Waterlily in Show, Cream of the Crop, and Fabulous Fifty. S. McClaren

610 'Taratahi Sunrise' (WL LB Y/OR, B. and J. Frater, 2001, New Zealand). Lynn B. Dudley Award. This perfect waterlily is bright yellow in the center blending to pastel orange in the margins. It is easy to grow on a healthy plant with many blooms. Ideal as a cut and show flower. Wins its Class, Best Single and Triple Waterlily in Show. ADS slide library

610 'Yume-Suiren' (WL LB Y/PK, Konishi, 1992, Japan) is pastel yellow blending to pink. The petal form is excellent, but it tends to have a greater depth than needed. It is easy to grow on a healthy plant with many early blooms. Good tuber production. Excellent cut and multiple flower for baskets. Wins its Class. Yusaku Konishi

611 'Kanzashi-Otome' (WL BR, Konishi, 1993, Japan) is blends of light bronze in the center to dark bronze at the margins. It has excellent petal form and is easy to grow. Long straight stems make it an excellent cut flower. Wins its Class. Yusaku Konishi

611 'Koppertone' (WL BR, Swan Island Dahlias, 1982, USA) is blends of yellow-bronze, an unusual color. It grows on a tall healthy plant with large blooms of great substance. A valuable addition to the cut flower ranks. Swan Island Dahlias

613 'Amy' (WL DB Y/DP, Tickner, 1963, Australia), a yellow center blending to a dark pink, is a small bloom with excellent stems. It is easy to grow on a healthy fully branched plant with many tubers. Wins its Class, Best Waterlily in Show, and Cream of the Crop. S. McClaren

613 'Ken's Rarity' (WL DB Y/W/PR, 1995, Farquhar, Australia) is pastel purple blending to white and yellow with a light reverse. It has perfect petals and form. Easy to grow on a wiry plant that needs staking. Wins its Class and Best Single and Triple Waterlily in Show. ADS slide library

612 'Ken's Flame' (WL FL, Farquhar, 1989, Australia) is bright yellow blending to a clear orange with perfect petals and form. Easy to grow on a healthy plant. Produces blooms on straight stems. Wins its Class, Best Single and Triple Waterlily in Show, and Cream of the Crop. Wayne Shantz

613 'DD Lee' (WL DB DP/Y, Diede, 2001, USA) is a dark blend with well-formed cupped petals. It is easy to grow on a healthy floriferous plant with good tuber formation. A very early bloom, and of firm substance—an excellent show and cut flower. Wins its Class, Best Single and Triple Waterlily in Show. McClaren

613 'Moray Susan' (WL DB DR/Y, McLaughlin, 1995*, Australia), an outstanding dark blend with excellent cupped petals and perfect form. Requires shade. Wins its Class and Cream of the Crop. Alan Fisher

613 'Sandia Calypso' (WL DB DP/Y, Boley, 2003, USA) has well-formed petals, bright yellow blending to a deep pink, and excellent form. It is easy to grow on a healthy plant with many blooms on erect stems. Valuable cut and show flower. Wins its Class.
Stephen L. Boley

614 'Heat Wave' (WL V Y/OR, 1995*) is bright yellow with small orange markings. It grows on a healthy floriferous fully branched plant. Strong stems make it an attractive cut flower. Wins its Class. S. McClaren

614 'Jess-Stripes' (WL V Y/R, Suttell, 1997, Canada) is a bright yellow nearly covered with heavy red markings. Easy to grow with many blooms, it lights up the show table and is a favorite of gardeners. Wins its Class. S. McClaren

614 'G W's Richard M' (WL V OR/Y/R, Wolfe, 2000*, USA), a red with yellow and orange variegated markings, has cupped petals and perfect form. It is easy to grow on a healthy fully branched plant with many early blooms. Good seed parent. Wins in a competitive Class and Cream of the Crop. S. McClaren

615 'Pink Gingham' (WL BI PK/W, Swan Island Dahlias, 1987, USA) is bright pink with white tips. It grows on a tall floriferous plant on strong stems, making it a valuable cut, garden, and show flower. Wins its Class. Swan Island Dahlias

CHAPTER 6

Ball, Miniature Ball, Pompon, Stellar, Novelty Fully Double

BALL

The ball dahlia is a fully double ball-shaped flower, slightly flattened at the face, having tightly rolled ray florets and a diameter over 3.5 in. (8.75 cm). Its perfect form and long shelf life make it ideal for the show table, cut flowers, formal floral designs, baskets, and bouquets.

The ball-shaped dahlia was one of the first dahlias grown in the early 1800s. The balls appearing in shows during the 19th century were called show, fancy, and ball dahlias at different times during the period. Its very formal appearance made the ball one of the most widely grown dahlias. In 1895 the ball was one of only four forms of dahlias being shown. In 1920 the ADS first classified the ball dahlia as a ball-shaped double dahlia. Later it was classified by size and ray floret formation. The photos in this section of the chapter represent 11 color classes.

BALL PHOTOS

501 'Brookside Snowball' (BA W, Hurt, 1976, USA), a large 5 in. (12.5 cm) ball, has been a favorite since its introduction. It is a clear clean white with round-tipped petals and perfect form. Many ideal blooms of great substance are carried on a tall healthy fully branched plant. Tolerates heat and is easy to grow, producing an abundance of tubers that keep well in storage. A perfect cut flower. Wins its Class, Best Ball in Show, Best Bloom of Show, Cream of the Crop, and Fabulous Fifty. ADS slide library

502 'Barbarry Yellow Cloud' (BA Y, Davies, 2000, UK). Lynn B. Dudley Award. This large bright yellow has well-formed petals and full petalage. It is easy to grow on a healthy plant with many early blooms held on strong straight stems; plants produce an abundance of tubers that keep in storage. Wins its Class, Best Single and Triple Ball in Show, and Cream of the Crop. McClaren

502 'Hy Maize' (BA Y, W. Holland, 2000, Canada), reclassified in 2003 from a BB formal decorative light blend, is golden yellow with round-tipped petals. It is easy to grow on a healthy fully branched plant with many early blooms and good tuber production; tubers keep well in storage. Firm substance and strong stems make it an excellent cut and show flower. Wins its Class. McClaren

503 'Barbarry Ball' (BA OR, Davies, 1991, UK). Lynn B. Dudley Award. This dahlia, a pale orange with full petalage, is borne on a healthy plant with excellent stems. Does well in a cool region with high humidity. Superior show and cut flower. Wins its Class. McClaren

505 'Celebrity Ball' (BA DP, L. Connell, 1990, USA) is clean pink with full petalage recurving to the stem. Easy to grow on a healthy plant with strong stems. Wins in a competitive Class and Best Ball in Show. McClaren

505 'Pink Robin Hood' (BA DP, 1994) is lavender-pink with well-formed petals and full petalage. It is easy to grow on a healthy floriferous plant. Wins its Class and Cream of the Crop. S. McClaren

506 'Camano Poppet' (BA R, R. Ambrose, 1979, USA) is nonfading bright red with blooms carried on long stems. It is easy to grow on a tall healthy plant with many long-keeping tubers. A valuable cut and show flower. Wins in a competitive Class. McClaren

507 'Cornel' (BA DR, Geerlings, 1994, Holland). Stanley Johnson Award. This excellent nonfading dark red is a perfectly formed ball. It grows on a strong fully branched plant with many early blooms and produces an abundance of tubers that keep well in long storage. Tolerates heat. Wins its Class, Best Single and Triple Ball in Show, Best Bloom in Show, Best Triple in Show, Cream of the Crop, and Fabulous Fifty. McClaren

507 'Paul Z' (BA DR, Larkin/Zydner, 2001, USA). Derrill W. Hart Award. This nonfading dark red with pointed petals performs well on the show table and as a cut flower. It has excellent form and is easy to grow; the tall healthy fully branched plant produces many early blooms. Wins its Class, Best Ball in Show, Best Bloom in Show, and Cream of the Crop. ADS slide library

508 'Hillcrest Bobbin' (BA L, Jackson, 1995*, UK) is clean lavender with pointed petals recurving to the stems. It is easy to grow on a healthy plant. Good substance and strong stems for cut and show blooms. Wins in a competitive Class. McClaren

508 'Kenora Tonya' (BA L, Leroux, 1990, USA) is clear lavender with full petalage. It grows on a healthy plant on strong stems. Wins in a competitive Class. McClaren

508 'Shirley Hudson' (BA L, L. Connell, 1982, USA) is clear lavender with firm substance. Valuable cut flower. Wins in a competitive Class. ADS slide library

509 'Aztec Bluebird' (BA PR, V. Hale, UK) is light purple with a darker reverse and full petalage recurving to the stem. It is easy to grow on a healthy plant. Good substance makes it a valuable cut and show flower. McClaren

509 'Hy Mallow' (BA PR, W. Holland, 2000, Canada). Derrill W. Hart Award. This lavender-purple ball with pointed petals grows on a tall healthy fully branched plant with many early blooms. Strong straight stems and firm substance make it an ideal show and cut flower. Wins in a competitive Class, Best Single and Triple Ball in Show, and Cream of the Crop. McClaren

510 'Senior Ball' (BA LB W/PR, Almand, 1980, USA). Derrill W. Hart Award. This dahlia, a white blending to pale purple, has extra-full petalage and grows on a healthy plant. Wins its Class, Best Ball in Show, and Cream of the Crop. McClaren

511 'Snoho Jo Jo' (BA BR, Bonneywell, 1990, USA). Derrill W. Hart Award. This bright yellow-bronze dahlia has pointed petals and full petalage recurved to the stem. It is an easy-to-grow flower with good substance, making it a valuable cut and show flower. Wins its Class, Best Ball in Show, and Cream of the Crop. McClaren

509 'Jessie G' (BA PR, L. Connell, 1994, USA). Derrill W. Hart and Stanley Johnson awards. A winner upon its introduction, this dahlia is easy to grow on a tall 6 ft. (1.8 m) healthy plant with full branching and many perfect dark blooms, with full petalage and well-formed petals. The stems are straight and long, making it a flower for all purposes. Wins its Class, Best Single and Triple Ball in Show, Best Single and Triple Bloom in Show, Cream of the Crop, and Fabulous Fifty. McClaren

510 'Suncrest' (BA LB Y/OR, Sampson, 1998*, Canada) is a perfectly named flower, a great blend of pale yellow and orange with well-formed petals and full petalage. Wins in a competitive Class, Best Ball in Show, and Cream of the Crop. Alan Fisher

513 'Robin Hood' (BA DB OR/PK, Littlejohn, 1987, UK) is bright orange blending to pink with full petalage. Easy to grow in all areas on a healthy well-branched plant with many blooms. Good tuber production. Wins its Class, Best Single and Triple Ball in Show, Cream of the Crop, and Fabulous Fifty. McClaren

MINIATURE BALL

The miniature ball dahlia is a fully double ball-shaped flower with tightly rolled ray florets. The ADS classifies the diameter of the flower from 2 to 3.5 in. (5 to 8.75 cm).

The miniature ball, with its perfect form, is used in the same way as the ball but is also popular as a dried flower.

Like other dahlia forms, the miniature ball has evolved during the 20th century. Originally, the miniature ball class included cultivars from the smallest balls, the largest pompons, and the miniatures, and in some countries there are still differences in its size. The photos in this section of the chapter represent 11 color classes.

522 'Hy Nugget' (MB Y, W. Holland, 2001, Canada) is bright yellow with full petalage recurved to the stem. It is easy to grow on a tall healthy plant with many early blooms. Wins in a competitive Class and Best Single Miniature Ball in Show. McClaren

522 'SB's Sunny' (MB Y, Boley, 2003, USA) is bright clean yellow with full petalage. It is easy to grow with many blooms on straight stems. Wins its Class and Best Single and Triple Miniature Ball in Show. Stephen L. Boley

521 'White Nettie' (MB W, 1974), a sport of 'Nettie', is a clean white with outstanding round petals and full petalage. It is easy to grow on a healthy floriferous plant with full branching and good tuber production; tubers store well. Wins its Class, Best Miniature Ball in Show, and Cream of the Crop. McClaren

522 'Nettie' (MB Y, Clarke, 1966, UK), a clean pale yellow, is the oldest miniature ball still being grown and winning. It has outstanding round petal form and is easy to grow on a healthy fully branched plant with many blooms. Wins its Class, Best Single and Triple Miniature Ball in Show, Cream of the Crop, and Fabulous Fifty. McClaren

523 'Ms Kennedy' (MB OR, Boley, 2002, USA) is brilliant orange with perfect petal form recurving to the stem. Strong straight stems and blooms of good substance make it a valuable cut and show flower. Wins its Class. Stephen L. Boley

525 'Mingus Gary' (MB DP, Mingus, 2001, USA) is dark pink with excellent rounded tight petals and full petalage. It is easy to grow on a healthy plant with many blooms. Wins its Class, Best Miniature Ball in Show, and Cream of the Crop. S. McClaren

526 'Hy Fire' (MB R, W. Holland, 1996, Canada), a nonfading red with pointed petals, is easy to grow on a tall healthy fully branched plant with many perfect blooms and tubers that store well. Straight strong stems make it an excellent cut and show flower. Wins its very competitive Class. McClaren

527 'Alpen Marc' (MB DR, McClaren, USA) is nonfading dark red, nearly black, with full petalage recurving to the stem. It grows on a tall fully branched plant with early blooms on long straight stems with firm substance. Wins its Class and Best Miniature Ball in Show. McClaren

526 'Alpen Dee' (MB R, McClaren, 1982, USA) is orange-red with a lighter reverse. It is easy to grow on a healthy plant with many early blooms. Wins in a very competitive Class. ADS slide library

526 'Red Admiral' (MB R, Long, 1982, UK), an excellent cut and basket flower with pointed petals, is easy to grow on a tall fully branched plant. Wins its Class, Best Single and Triple Miniature Ball in Show, Best Bloom in Show, Cream of the Crop, and Fabulous Fifty. McClaren

527 'Aurora's Kiss' (MB DR, W. Holland, 1997, Canada) is nonfading blends of dark red, nearly black—a desirable color—with loosely rolled petal form. Strong straight stems make it an attractive show and cut flower. Wins its Class and Cream of the Crop. McClaren

527 'Barbarry Gem' (MB DR, Davies, 1990, UK). Lynn B. Dudley Award. With very tightly rolled petals, reflexed ray florets, and full petalage, this easy-to-grow dahlia is the standard for miniature balls. Perfect blooms appear in mid season on a tall healthy floriferous plant; the many tubers produced keep well in storage. Prefers cool climates with humidity. Wins its Class, Best Single and Triple Miniature Ball in Show, Cream of the Crop, and Fabulous Fifty. McClaren

527 'Mary Karen Z' (MB DR, Zatkovich, 1989, USA) is dark red with pointed petals and excellent form. Does well in midwestern United States and Canada. Wins its Class and Best Single and Triple Miniature Ball in Show. Ben Bartel

528 'Robann Royal' (MB L, Moynahan, 1991, USA). Derrill W. Hart Award. This dahlia, lavender blends with fully rolled pointed petals, grows on a fully branched floriferous plant. Wins its Class, Best Miniature Ball in Show, Cream of the Crop, and Fabulous Fifty. McClaren

529 'Chimicum Troy' (MB PR, D. and L. Smith, 2003, USA). Lynn B. Dudley Award. This nearly black dark purple with full petalage is proving itself as a single and multiple show flower. Excellent for baskets. Wins in a very competitive Class, Best Miniature Ball in Show, and Cream of the Crop. McClaren

529 'Downham Royal' (MB PR, Sharp, 1972, UK), a dark purple with perfect form, has been winning since its introduction. It has correctly proportioned straight stems with firm substance, making it a great cut flower. Wins its Class, Best Single and Triple Miniature Ball in Show, Best Bloom in Show, Cream of the Crop, and Fabulous Fifty. McClaren

529 'Woodland's Dufus' (MB PR, Mishler, 2002, USA) is reddish purple with excellent form. Wins its Class and Best Single and Triple Miniature Ball in Show. ADS slide library

531 'Buffie G' (MB BR, Swan Island Dahlias, 1992, USA), a bronze with a reverse of mauve tones, is easy to grow on a healthy mid-sized well-branched plant with many blooms. Sometimes grown as a pompon. Makes attractive baskets. Swan Island Dahlias

534 'Alpen Marjory' (MB V L/R/Y, McClaren, 1986, USA) is lavender with markings of red and yellow—a different look. It has excellent formation and is easy to grow, with many early blooms and tubers that survive long storage. Excellent seed parent. Wins its Class, Best Miniature Ball in Show, and Cream of the Crop. McClaren

531 'Hy Suntan' (MB BR, W. Holland, 2000, Canada) is a rich warm bronze with well-formed petals and full petalage. It is easy to grow on a tall healthy fully branched plant. Produces many early blooms and excellent tubers; tubers keep well in storage. Wins its Class, Best Single and Triple Miniature Ball in Show, and Cream of the Crop. McClaren

533 Seedling (MB DB PR/W, Boley, USA) is a dark blend with full petalage recurving to the stem. It is easy to grow with firm substance. Wins its Class. Stephen L. Boley

POMPON

The pompon dahlia is one of the smallest dahlias. The diameter of the flower is less than 2 in. (5 cm). The form is a fully double flower with tightly rolled ray florets. Even though the flowers are small, the usual plant height is from 3 to 4 ft. (0.9 to 1.2 m).

The pompon's diminutive size makes it ideal for bud vases, corsages, and small bouquets. It is the favored dahlia for drying.

The pompon was grown in England and Germany in the early to mid-19th century. It has been known as Lilliputian, Lilliput, bouquet, and pompone. As early as 1895 it was grown in the United States and has been listed as a form since. This form should be a focus of hybridizers: very few pompons have been developed in the past several decades. The photos in this section of the chapter represent ten color classes.

542 'Yellow Baby' (P Y, Lammerse, 1960, Holland), a yellow with perfectly formed petals, is one of the easiest pompons to cultivate in all areas. It grows on a healthy fully branched plant with many early blooms and produces excellent tubers that store well for a long period. Tolerates heat. Wins its Class, Best Single and Triple Pompon in Show, Cream of the Crop, and Fabulous Fifty. McClaren

543 'Poppet' (P OR, Ballego, 1969, Holland), a yellow-orange with an excellent center and perfect form, has won more awards than any other pompon. It grows on a small plant and blooms from mid to late season. Does well in all areas and tolerates heat. Wins its Class, Best Single and Triple Pompon in Show, Cream of the Crop, and Fabulous Fifty. S. McClaren

541 'Small World' (P W, N. Williams, 1967*, Australia), a pure white, has a small tip on the end of each petal and full petalage with excellent form. At times considered identical to 'Bowen'. It is easy to grow on a healthy fully branched plant with many tubers that keep well in storage. Wins its Class, Best Single and Triple Pompon in Show, and Cream of the Crop. S. McClaren

543 'Chimicum Pumpkin' (P OR, D. and L. Smith, 1999, USA). Lynn B. Dudley Award. This red-orange with well-formed petals is one of the larger pompons. It has small tubers, prefers shade, and is easy to grow on a small plant. Tolerates heat and does well throughout the United States and Canada. Wins its Class, Best Single and Triple Pompon in Show, and Cream of the Crop. McClaren

544 'Dutch Baby' (P PK, Geerlings, 1988, Holland) is a soft pale pink with a well-formed center, full petalage, and perfect form. Easy to grow on a fully branched plant with many blooms. Wins its Class, Best Single and Triple Pompon of the Show, and Cream of the Crop. S. McClaren

545 'Hallmark' (P DP, N. Williams, 1960, Australia) is dark lavender-pink with ideal form, excellent pleated petals, and a perfectly formed center. Grows best from pot tubers since tubers have a short storage period. Wins its Class, Best Single and Triple Pompon, Cream of the Crop, and Fabulous Fifty. S. McClaren

548 'Frank Holmes' (P L, F. Holmes, 1976, UK) was reclassified in 2003 from pink to lavender. It is easy to grow on a healthy fully branched plant with many early blooms. Tolerates heat and produces an abundance of tubers that keep well in storage. Wins in a competitive Class, Best Single and Triple Pompon in Show, and Cream of the Crop. McClaren

548 'Lilac Willo' (P L, 1978*), with perfect form and full petalage, is easy to grow on a healthy fully branched plant with many blooms. Wins in a very competitive Class, Best Single and Triple Pompon in Show. S. McClaren

546 'Red Carol' (P R, 2002*), a brilliant red with well-formed petals and long straight stems, is easy to grow on a healthy plant. Heat can cause the petals to be notched. Grows best from cuttings since tubers do not keep well in storage. Wins its competitive Class. McClaren

548 'Koko Puff' (P L, Swan Island Dahlias, 1994, USA) is smoky lavender with small blooms and full petalage. It grows on a healthy compact plant. Wins its Class and Best Pompon in Show. Swan Island Dahlias

548 'Mark Lockwood' (P L, Lockwood, 1974, UK) is dark lavender with pointed petals and excellent form. It is easy to grow on a healthy fully branched plant with many early blooms. Produces an abundance of tubers that have a long storage life. Tolerates heat. Wins its Class, Best Single and Triple Pompon in Show, and Cream of the Crop. S. McClaren

549 'Moor Place' (P PR, Newnham, 1955, UK) was reclassified from dark red to purple in 2002. Considered identical to 'Glenplace' by some, but others can discern differences in the plant and tuber growth. It has excellent form and is easy to grow on a fully branched plant; the stems of the many early blooms are often short but have good growth later. Tolerates heat and produces an abundance of tubers that keep well in storage. Wins in two very competitive classes, Best Single and Triple Pompon in Show, Cream of the Crop, and Fabulous Fifty. McClaren

549 'Oreti Duke' (P PR, W. Jack, 1990, New Zealand) is blends of purple with full petalage recurving to the stem. It is easy to grow on a tall fully branched plant with many early blooms. Firm substance and strong straight stems make it a cut and show flower. Wins its Class, Best Single and Triple Pompon in Show, and Cream of the Crop. Walter Jack

549 'SB's Dandy' (P PR, Boley, 2003, USA) is dark purple with petals recurving to the stem. It is easy to grow on a healthy plant with many blooms on sturdy stems. Wins its Class.
Stephen L. Boley

550 'Gurtla Twilight' (P LB W/PR, Wilkinson, 1996, UK) is white blending to a dark purple on the edges and the notched tips. Full petalage. Prefers cool climates and humidity. Wins its Class and Cream of the Crop. S. McClaren

550 'Mi Wong' (P LB L/W, 1976*, UK), originally classified as dark pink, was reclassified as a light blend in 1999. The color varies; in cool weather with humidity and shade, the color is outstanding. With full petalage and excellent form, it wins its Class, Best Single and Triple Pompon in Show, and Cream of the Crop. S. McClaren

552 'Lismore Sunset' (P FL, W. Franklin, 1998, UK) is clean yellow blending to bright red tips with excellent form and petals recurving to the stem. It is easy to grow on a healthy plant with many early blooms. Wins its Class, Best Single and Triple Pompon in Show. McClaren

STELLAR

The stellar dahlia is fully double with narrow involute ray florets slightly recurved to the stem. The depth of the flower should be from ½ to ⅔ the diameter of the flower.

Prior to 1983, it was not possible to introduce dahlias that did not meet the requirements of one of the recognized forms. A new classification, novelty, was created by the ADS for classifying dahlias with characteristics distinct and different from present forms. This made it possible for hybridizers to develop entirely new dahlias and have them classified. In 2002 the novelty class was divided into three new classes: novelty fully double, novelty open center, and stellar. Imports and new introductions of stellar dahlias have produced adequate numbers for a permanent listing in the *ADS Classification and Handbook of Dahlias*. The stellar has been a popular flower in Australia but very few countries have recognized the form.

The stellar has been referred to as the "double orchid," because its petal formation is similar to the orchid form. The flower is used as a cut and show flower and in artistic designs. The photos in this section of the chapter represent seven color classes.

562 'Juugoya-Otome' (ST Y, Konishi, Japan) is bright yellow with excellent form. It is easy to grow on a strong healthy plant with good tuber production. Wins its Class. Yusaku Konishi

563 'Crazy Legs' (ST OR, Swan Island Dahlias, 1990, USA), originally a novelty but reclassified as a stellar in 2002, is burnt apricot with a reverse of dutch-vermilion and full petalage. It is easy to grow on a healthy fully branched plant with many blooms. With firm substance and well-proportioned stems, it is a successful show and cut flower. Wins its Class. Swan Island Dahlias

563 'Kid's Stuff' (ST OR, Swan Island Dahlias, 2003, USA) is orange with small notches on the tips. It is easy to grow on a healthy plant with many blooms held on strong straight stems. A valuable cut flower. Should win its Class. Swan Island Dahlias

564 'Alloway Candy' (ST PK, Stitt, 1988*, New Zealand), originally a novelty but reclassified as a stellar in 2002, is pastel pink on the face and reverse. It has excellent petal form and full petalage and is easy to grow in all areas. Many early blooms are borne on a tall healthy fully branched plant that produces an abundance of tubers; tubers keep well in storage. Tolerates heat. Firm substance and well-proportioned stems make it a great show and cut flower. Wins its Class, Best Single and Triple Stellar in Show, Best Bloom in Show, Cream of the Crop, and Fabulous Fifty. McClaren

565 'Mingus Denise' (ST DP, Mingus, 1999, USA), a petite bloom, is dark pink on the face and reverse. Originally a novelty, it was reclassified as a stellar in 2002. It grows on a short plant, well branched with many blooms. Wins its Class and Cream of the Crop. McClaren

569 'Raspberry Punch' (ST PR, Swan Island Dahlias, 2002, USA) has ideal stellar petals rolling toward the stem. It grows on a tall healthy plant with blooms of firm substance. Introduced as a B but reclassified as a stellar within the year. A valuable cut and show flower.
Swan Island Dahlias

569 Seedling (ST PR, McClaren, USA) is a clean reddish purple with well-formed petals. A healthy plant with many early blooms, it should win its Class.
McClaren

570 'Camano Pet' (ST LB Y/OR, R. Ambrose, 1997, USA), originally a novelty but reclassified as a stellar in 2002, is a blend: pastel yellow in the center, pastel orange toward the margins of the bloom. It grows well from pot tubers in all areas on a tall healthy fully branched plant with many perfect blooms. Tolerates heat. Strong well-proportioned stems make it a perfect show, cut, and basket flower. Wins its Class, Best Single and Triple Stellar in Show, Cream of the Crop, and Fabulous Fifty. Jim Rowse

573 'Fidalgo Julie' (ST DB OR/R, Matthies, 1988, USA). Derrill W. Hart Award. Originally a novelty, this stellar was reclassified in 2002. It is orange blending to red on the face and red blending to orange on the reverse—a brilliant combination, and a great cut, basket, arranger, and show flower, with firm substance and strong stems. Easy to grow with many blooms. Wins its Class, Best Single and Triple Stellar in Show, Cream of the Crop, and Fabulous Fifty.
ADS slide library

573 'Jescot Julie' (ST DB OR/PR, Cooper, 1974, UK) is orange on the face and purple on the reverse. Introduced as a peony in 1988, it was first changed to a novelty and then in 2002 to a stellar. It is easy to grow with many blooms and has many uses, as a cut, arranger, collection, and show flower. Wins its Class, Best Single and Triple Stellar in Show, and Cream of the Crop. ADS slide library

NOVELTY FULLY DOUBLE PHOTOS

NOVELTY FULLY DOUBLE

The novelty fully double dahlia has closed centers and characteristics that do not fit the requirements of any other fully double classification. This is a new form, listed by the ADS for the first time in 2002. The photos in this section of the chapter represent eight color classes.

781 'Horse Feathers' (NX W, Geisert, 1995, USA), a pure white with many notched and laciniated petals and full petalage, was reclassified from a novelty to a novelty fully double in 2002. It grows on a healthy fully branched plant with many blooms. Does best in cool climates with high humidity. Wins its Class, Best Novelty Fully Double in Show, Cream of the Crop, and Fabulous Fifty. McClaren

786 'Akita' (NX R, Konishi, 1989, Japan) is an unusual bloom with red chrysanthemum-like petals with incurved white tips. It was reclassified from a novelty to a novelty fully double in 2002. Blooms mid to late season on a strong plant with sturdy stems. Stock is difficult to locate. Wins its Class, Best Novelty Fully Double in Show, and Cream of the Crop. Yusaku Konishi

787 'Akita No Hikari' (NX DR, Ohta, 1981, Japan) has dark red chrysanthemum-like petals with incurved white tips. Blooms prolifically mid to late season on a tall healthy plant. It was reclassified from a novelty to a novelty fully double in 2002. Easy to grow and produces many tubers that keep well in storage. Wins its Class, Best Single and Triple Novelty Fully Double in Show, Cream of the Crop, and Fabulous Fifty. McClaren

789 'Optic Illusion' (NX PR, Swan Island Dahlias, 1992, USA) has rose-purple formal decorative petals with white petaloids interspersed between each ray floret. Originally classified as a B formal decorative but changed to a novelty in 1996, and again to a novelty fully double in 2002. It grows from small tubers on a tall healthy plant with blooms on strong stems. A valuable cut and show flower. Wins its Class as a Single and Triple and as Best Novelty Fully Double in Show. Swan Island Dahlias

789 'Shinkyoku' (NX PR, Ohta, 1970, Japan) is reddish purple with tightly revolute cactus petals with tiny white tips. It is easy to grow on a healthy plant with many mid to late blooms; stems of the first blooms tend to be short but are in proportion to the flower by the second blooms. Reclassified from a B incurved cactus to a novelty fully double in 2002. A great flower for artistic designs. Wins its Class, Best Single and Triple Novelty Fully Double, and Cream of the Crop. Yusaku Konishi

790 'Valley Porcupine' (NX LB W/PK, D. and L. Smith, 2002*, USA), a white blending to pink on the outer edges of each petal, is a new petal form with involute petals attached at both ends. It grows on a healthy plant with great substance and perfectly proportioned stems. An ideal novelty fully double flower. Wins its Class, Best Single and Triple Novelty Fully Double in Show, Best Bloom in Show, Cream of the Crop, and Fabulous Fifty. McClaren

791 'Thistle' (NX BR, Sell, 1985*, USA) is aptly named for its thistle-like appearance. Tends to have an open center, but when well developed its form is excellent; it has been a consistent winner since the novelty class was established. Wins its Class as a Single and Triple, Best Novelty Fully Double in Show, People's Choice, and Cream of the Crop. Dick Ambrose

794 'Be-A-Sport' (NX V OR/R/w, Swan Island Dahlias, 1992, USA), a sport of 'Candy Cane', is an unusual variegated dahlia, orange with red splashes and perfect white tips. It grows on a healthy well-branched plant with many blooms. A good cut, bouquet, basket, and show flower. Swan Island Dahlias

791 Seedling (NX BR, McClaren, USA), a pale bronze with a pink blush, is a new petal form with involute petals attached at both ends and full petalage recurving to the stem. It is an easy plant to grow with many early blooms. With strong straight stems and good substance, it will be a valuable cut and show flower. Wins its Class, Best Single and Triple Novelty Fully Double in Show. McClaren

792 Seedling (NX FL DR/Y, McClaren, USA) is dark red with bright yellow tips on notched petals. All ray florets are tubular as it opens, becoming flat as they develop. It grows on a healthy plant with strong stems. McClaren

794 'Mads' (NX V DP/DR/w, Gregersdal, Denmark) is a BB size dark pink with dark red markings and even white tips, both variegated and bicolor. It grows on a healthy plant with strong stems. Tubers do not keep long in storage, but it takes excellent cuttings, which produce excellent plants. Wins its Class and Best Novelty Fully Double in Show. McClaren

CHAPTER 7

Single, Mignon Single, Collarette, Orchid, Peony, Anemone, Novelty Open

SINGLE

The single dahlia is an open-centered dahlia with a single row of uniform, evenly spaced ray florets in a flat plane surrounding the disc flowers. The size is 2 in. (5 cm) and over.

The earliest recognized *Dahlia* species were open-centered flowers, making the single one of the earliest dahlia forms. In some areas of the world the single form is not a recognized class, and many ADS shows did not have a single class until the late 1970s. The ADS now recommends that all ADS shows include a class for every recognized form. The simplicity of the single dahlia makes it ideal for use in artistic floral designs. The photos in this section of the chapter represent eight color classes.

SINGLE PHOTOS

706 'Alta Bishop' (S R/y, Mason/Yano, 1968, USA) is bright red with a yellow eye-zone. It has round petals, uniformly shaped, and is easy to grow on a healthy plant with many blooms. Good tuber production. Wins its Class, Best Single and Triple Single in Show, and Cream of the Crop. McClaren

708 'Dizzy' (S L/dr, Swan Island Dahlias, 1999, USA) is dark lavender with a dark red eye-zone. It is easy to grow on a healthy plant. Stems are straight and long, making it a good cut flower. Swan Island Dahlias

710 Seedling (S LB W/L/y, McClaren, USA) is white with brushstrokes of pastel lavender on the center and a yellow eye-zone. Large blooms are carried on long stems on a tall healthy plant. Wins its Class and Best Single and Triple in Show. McClaren

708 'Alpen Matthew' (S L/dr, McClaren, 2004, USA) is clean sharp lavender with a dark red eye-zone and perfect petal form. It is easy to grow on a healthy plant with many early blooms. Great stems and firm substance. Wins its Class and Best Single and Triple Single Bloom in Show. McClaren

709 Seedling (S PR, McClaren, USA) is brilliant purple with pleated petals. It grows on a healthy plant with many very early blooms. Wins its Class and Best Single and Triple Single in Show. McClaren

710 Seedling (S LB Y/R, McClaren, USA) is a large single with well-formed petalage and a bright yellow center blending to shades of red on the face. Blooms prolifically and early on a tall healthy plant with strong straight stems. Wins its Class, Best Single and Triple Single in Show. McClaren

711 'Alpen Aztec' (S BR, McClaren, 2003, USA) is yellow-bronze with round petals. It is easy to grow, producing many very early blooms and an abundance of tubers that keep well in storage. Wins its Class. McClaren

711 Seedling (S BR/dr, McClaren, USA) is a striking pastel yellow-bronze with a dark red eye-zone and well-formed petals. Wins its Class. McClaren

713 'Bashful' (S DB PR/L, Swan Island Dahlias, 1999, USA) is dark purple blending to lavender tips. It grows on a short floriferous plant. The small blooms have a good shelf life and are useful in small baskets and bouquets. Swan Island Dahlias

711 'Moonfire' (S BR/r, 1998*) is yellow-bronze with a red eye-zone and round evenly shaped petals. Blooms are carried on strong straight stems on a healthy floriferous dark-foliaged plant. Easy to grow. Wins its Class and Best Single and Triple Single in Show. McClaren

713 'Alpen Dusk' (S DB R/dr, McClaren, 1997, USA) is nonfading red blending to a dark red eye-zone. This perfectly formed single is easy to grow on a healthy plant with many early blooms. It has good tuber production; tubers keep well in storage. Wins its Class and Best Single and Triple Single in Show. McClaren

713 'Buffalo Nan' (S DB PR/l, J. Hart, 1998, USA) is reddish purple blending to lavender, with rounded petals. It grows on a healthy plant with many early blooms. Excellent tuber production. Good substance, a good cut and show flower. Wins its Class. McClaren

713 'CG Eclipse' (S DB R/y, Larkin/ Zydner, 2002, USA) is a showstopper that could easily be a bicolor, a bright nonfading red with yellow tips and perfectly formed round petals. Easy to grow on a healthy plant with many early blooms. Wins its Class and Best Single and Triple Single in Show. McClaren

713 Seedling (S DB W/pr, Kestell, USA) is clean white blending to brushstrokes of dark purple in the center of the bloom. Excellent petal form. Blooms prolifically and early on straight stems on a tall healthy plant. Wins its Class. McClaren

714 Seedling (S V OR/r, McClaren, USA), a bright orange with red markings, grows on a tall plant with many large blooms on great stems. Needed in its class. Wins Best Single and Triple Single Bloom in Show. McClaren

713 'Mii Tai' (S DB W/PR, McClaren, 1999, USA) is white outlined in reddish purple blending to a reddish purple eyezone. It has round petals and is easy to grow on a healthy plant. The many early blooms are carried on strong straight stems. Outstanding seed parent. Wins its Class, Best Single and Triple Single in Show, and Cream of the Crop. McClaren

713 Seedling (S DB DR/L, McClaren, USA) is dark red blending to lavender tips on flat petals. Many early blooms of firm substance are carried on a healthy plant. Wins its Class, Best Single and Triple Single in Show. McClaren

715 'Alpen Shadows' (S BI DR/l, McClaren, 2000, USA) is dark red with lavender tips and large perfectly formed blooms of firm substance. It is easy to grow with many early blooms and an abundance of tubers that keep well in storage. Wins its Class, Best Single and Triple Single in Show, and Cream of the Crop. McClaren

715 Seedling (S BI R/pk, McClaren, USA) has well-formed petals and good substance. It is easy to grow on a tall healthy plant with early blooms on sturdy stems. Wins Best Single and Triple Single in Show. McClaren

715 Seedling (S BI DR/l, McClaren, USA) is dark red with pale lavender tips. It grows on a healthy plant with many early blooms and good substance. Wins its Class, Best Single and Triple Single in Show. McClaren

MIGNON SINGLE

The mignon single dahlia is the same as the single dahlia except the size is less than 2 in. (5 cm), making it one of the smallest dahlias.

The first record (circa late 1800s) of the mignon single describes it as being grown in Holland on plants 4 to 5 ft. (1.2 to 1.5 m) tall. Later, the Tom Thumb plants, which were 8 to 15 in. (20 to 37.5 cm), appeared, and for years the mignon single was grown primarily as a dwarf under 12 in. (30 cm); however, taller plants are again being grown. The mignon single has an inconsistent classification history, and at one time was shown as a subclass of the single. As early as 1971 it was listed in the ADS classification as dwarf mignon; since 1977 it has been listed as mignon single. Throughout its history, the mignon single has gone by several different names: miniature, Tom Thumb, Lilliput, topmix, dwarf single, bedding dahlia, and dwarf mignon.

The mignon single is the most popular dahlia for use as a border plant. As a low-growing plant, it is ideal for windy areas, and it is also used for drying, window boxes, potted plants, miniature designs, and baskets. Because of its near perfect form it can win higher awards at dahlia shows. The photos in this section of the chapter represent ten color classes.

721 'Lupin Tori' (MS W/y, B. Jones, 1997, USA). Lynn B. Dudley Award. This dahlia is white with a small yellow eye-zone and involute pointed evenly spaced petals of the same shape in a flat plane. Blooms are near maximum size. Easy to grow on a healthy floriferous plant. Produces an abundance of tubers that keep well in storage. Wins its Class, Best Single and Triple Mignon Single in Show, Cream of the Crop, and Fabulous Fifty. McClaren

722 'CG Charm' (MS Y, Larkin/Zydner, 2002, USA) is brilliant yellow with flat round petals. It has strong stems and grows on a healthy plant with many blooms. Wins its Class. McClaren

722 'Topmix Yellow' (MS Y, Ballego, 1967, Holland) has clear bright yellow petals. It is easy to grow on a low-growing plant with many blooms, making it a valuable potted plant. Wins its Class and Best Single and Triple Mignon Single in Show. McClaren

723 'Inflammation' (MS OR, Ballego, 1961, Holland) is a blend of orange with a dark orange eye-zone and pleated petals. Large blooms are carried on a sturdy plant on strong straight stems. Easy to grow, tolerates heat. Wins its Class, Best Single and Multiple Mignon Single in Show, Best Bloom in Show, Best Potted Plant in Show, Cream of the Crop, and Fabulous Fifty. McClaren

723 'Matthew Juul' (MS OR/dr, Juul, 1996, USA). Lynn B. Dudley and Derrill W. Hart awards. This dahlia, an orange with a dark-red eye-zone and perfectly round petals, was reclassified from a dark blend to an orange in 2003. It is easy to grow on a healthy plant with many perfect blooms. The abundance of tubers produced keep well in storage. Wins its Class, Best Single and Multiple Mignon Single in Show, Cream of the Crop, and Fabulous Fifty. S. McClaren

724 'Exotic Dwarf' (MS PK/pr, Nuyens, 1965, Holland) is lavender-pink with a reddish purple blush blending to a reddish purple eye-zone with round notched petals. It was reclassified from a dark blend to pink in 2003. Wins its Class, Best Single and Triple Mignon Single in Show, and Cream of the Crop. Jim Rowse

725 'Bonne Esperance' (MS DP, Topsvoort, 1948, Holland) is a clean lavender-pink with well-formed petals. Easy to grow. Blooms prolifically on a healthy low-growing plant throughout the season. The tubers keep in long storage. When well grown it tends to be oversized. Wins its Class, Best Single and Triple Mignon Single in Show. McClaren

726 Seedling (MS R, McClaren) is bright red with well-spaced petals. Blooms very early and prolifically on a low-growing plant with strong stems. Easy to grow and makes an excellent pot plant, covered with flowers throughout the season. Wins its Class. McClaren

727 'Rembrandt' (MS DR, Libert, 1989*, USA), a dark red blending to a darker red eye-zone, has perfect small blooms with ideal form. It is easy to grow on dwarf plants with many early blooms and well-proportioned stems. Produces an abundance of tubers that keep well in long storage. Makes an ideal potted plant. Wins its Class, Best Single and Multiple Bloom in Show, Best Bloom in Show, Best Basket in Show, Best Potted Plant in Show, Cream of the Crop, and Fabulous Fifty. McClaren

732 Seedling (MS FL/DR/Y, McClaren, USA), a dark red blending to yellow, has pointed petals and grows on a short healthy plant with many early small blooms and strong stems. Excellent potted plant. Wins its Class. McClaren

734 Seedling (MS V OR/R, McClaren, USA) is bright orange with red markings. Many early blooms are carried on a short bushy plant that is easy to disbud. Wins its Class, Best Single and Triple Mignon Single in Show. McClaren

733 'Daisy' (MS DB PK/DR, H. Miller, 1985*, USA) is pink with a blush of red blending to a dark red. It is easy to grow with many blooms and makes an excellent show and potted flower. Does well in all climates and tolerates heat. Wins its Class, Best Single and Triple Mignon Single in Show, Best Potted Plant in Show, and Cream of the Crop. McClaren

731 'Alpen Hazel' (MS BR, McClaren, 2003, USA) is yellowish bronze with round petals. It grows on a healthy plant with many tubers that keep well in storage. It is needed in its class. McClaren

COLLARETTE

The collarette dahlia is an open-centered dahlia with a single row of uniform compound florets composed of petaloids and ray florets surrounding the disc flower. It was hybridized in the early 1900s in France and Germany. The name came from the collar surrounding the disc flower. The collarette first appeared in the United States in 1912; in 1915 the ADS listed the collarette as a form. The photos in this section of the chapter represent 13 color classes.

662 Seedling (CO Y/y, McClaren, USA), a pastel yellow with pastel petaloids, has well-formed petals with evenly spaced petaloids ½ the length of the petals. It is easy to grow on a tall healthy plant with many early blooms of firm substance. Wins its Class and Best Single and Triple Collarette in Show. McClaren

663 'Giggles' (CO OR/pr, Swan Island Dahlias, 1998, USA) has petals evenly spaced in a flat plane with extra-long light rose-purple petaloids. It grows on a healthy plant with many blooms. Wins its Class and Best Collarette in Show. Swan Island Dahlias

661 'Alpen Cherub' (CO W/w, McClaren, 1987, USA) has pleated white slightly overlapping round petals with white petaloids uniformly ½ the length of the petals in a flat plane. Many early blooms are borne on a healthy fully branched plant. It is easy to grow and produces an abundance of tubers that keep well in storage. Excellent basket flower, grows in all areas, and tolerates heat. Wins its Class, Best Single and Triple Collarette in Show, Cream of the Crop, and Fabulous Fifty. McClaren

662 'Yellow Bird' (CO Y/w, 1976*) is clear yellow with white petaloids in a flat plane. An excellent form that shows well. Wins its Class. Wayne Shantz

664 'Jazzy' (CO PK/pk/w, Swan Island Dahlias, 1996, USA) is bright fluorescent pink blending to darker pink in the center. Petals are in a flat plane, and petaloids are pink blending to white, with an ideal length. It grows on a healthy plant with many blooms. Wins its Class. Swan Island Dahlias

666 'Caboose' (CO R/y/r, Swan Island Dahlias, 1996, USA) is flashy red with large uneven petaloids of yellow with red splashes. It grows on a healthy plant with many long-lasting blooms. Wins its very competitive Class and Best Collarette in Show. Swan Island Dahlias

666 'Mr. Jones' (CO R/r/w, Morin, 1999, USA). Lynn B. Dudley Award. This is a brilliant red dahlia with well-formed pointed evenly spaced petals in a flat plane and red and white petaloids. Easy to grow on a small plant. Wins its Class, Best Single and Triple Collarette in Show. McClaren

666 'Thriller' (CO R/r/w, Swan Island Dahlias, 1996, USA) has deep red petals evenly spaced and on a plane with red and white petaloids. An attractive garden flower with many blooms. Wins its Class. Swan Island Dahlias

666 'Mickey' (CO R/db/r/w, Swan Island Dahlias, 1989, USA) has velvety red petals evenly spaced on a flat plane; the petaloids are red blending to white, and not always of the same size. Blooms prolifically and early on a healthy plant. Wins its Class. Swan Island Dahlias

666 'My Joy' (CO R/y, Swan Island Dahlias, 1991, USA) has dusty rose petals with pastel yellow petaloids. The crowded petals are of different shapes, with some out of plane; the petaloids too are variously shaped, with some too long. Grows on a tall healthy plant. An attractive garden flower. Swan Island Dahlias

666 'Wheels' (CO R/y, Swan Island Dahlias, 1996, USA) is a vivid splash of nonfading red with well-formed evenly shaped overlapping petals and bright yellow petaloids ¾ the length of the petals in a flat plane. Easy to grow on a well-branched plant with many blooms. Wins its Class, Best Single Collarette in Show, and Cream of the Crop. S. McClaren

666 'Wowie' (CO R/lb/r/w, Swan Island Dahlias, 2001, USA) is a brilliant red-orange with petals that tend to be crowded and not always in a flat plane; the large evenly shaped petaloids are white with a blush of red. Blooms of great substance are carried on strong stems on a healthy plant. A good cut and show flower. Wins its Class.
Swan Island Dahlias

668 'Mary Layton' (CO L/w/w, Kutschara, 1991, USA) is lavender blending to white with white petaloids. The petals are in a flat plane, and the petaloids are evenly spaced. It is easy to grow on a healthy plant with many early blooms. Wins in a competitive Class and Best Single and Triple Collarette in Show. ADS slide library

669 'Alpen Flathead' (CO PR v/pr/w, McClaren, 1997, USA) has evenly spaced round purple petals with variegated markings, purple with white, on the petaloids, which are ⅔ the length of the petals in a flat plane. It is an easy flower to grow on a healthy plant with many early blooms. Produces an abundance of tubers that keep well in storage. Wins its Class and Best Single and Triple Collarette in Show. McClaren

667 'Pipsqueak' (CO DR/db/r/w, Swan Island Dahlias, 1998, USA) has watermelon-rose petals sometimes crowded with blended white and red petaloids. It grows on a healthy plant with blooms that are well suited for bouquets and arrangements. Swan Island Dahlias

668 'Rosy Wings' (CO L/pk, Swan Island Dahlias, 1990, USA) is lavender-pink, with some petals out of plane, with pink petaloids. It grows on a healthy plant with blooms of good substance and strong stems, making it a valuable cut and show flower. Wins its Class and Best Single and Triple Collarette in Show. Swan Island Dahlias

669 'Bee Happy' (CO PR/pr/pr, Swan Island Dahlias, 2001, USA) is a unique shade of purple with a dark purple eye-zone and small uneven purple petaloids. The disc flower is very dark. Stems and foliage too are dark, bringing striking contrast to the garden.
Swan Island Dahlias

669 'Mz. Bee Haven' (CO PR/db/pr/w, Swan Island Dahlias, 2003, USA) has bright purple petals, which may be out of plane, with purple and white blend petaloids. The compact low-growing plant does well in containers and borders. Swan Island Dahlias

670 'Alpen Lois' (CO LB PK/Y/w/l, McClaren, 2001, USA) has round evenly spaced petals, a blend of pink and yellow; petaloids are a blend of white and lavender and are uniformly ½ the length of the petals. It is easy to grow on a tall healthy fully branched plant with many perfect early blooms on strong straight stems. The many tubers produced store well for long periods. Firm substance makes it an excellent basket and bouquet flower. Wins its Class, Best Single and Triple Collarette in Show, and Cream of the Crop. McClaren

670 'Bumble Rumble' (CO LB DP/P/w, Swan Island Dahlias, USA) is a unique color combination—petals of dark pink outlined with a wide border of pastel pink with a reverse of dark pink, with large white petaloids nearly covering the petals—and the form is so different, it could easily be classified as a novelty open. It grows on a healthy plant that blooms prolifically throughout the season. Wins its Class and Best Collarette in Show. Swan Island Dahlias

670 'Easter Bonnet' (CO LB L/W/lb/w/l, Swan Island Dahlias, 2002, USA) has well-formed round petals, evenly overlapping and in attractive blends of white with light pale lavender, with petaloids ½ the length of the petal, pale lavender blending to white. An attractive collarette, appropriately named. Swan Island Dahlias

670 'Alpen Diamond' (CO LB L/W/lb/l/w, McClaren, 2004, USA). Evie Gullikson awards (trial gardens, seedling bench). This dahlia is pastel lavender blending to white in the center; each ray floret is outlined in purple with evenly spaced petaloids of white blending to lavender; petals are well formed and in a flat plane. Easy to grow on a tall healthy plant covered with early blooms on long straight stems. Wins its Class and Best Single and Triple Collarette in Show. McClaren

ORCHID

The orchid dahlia is open-centered with a single row of ray florets surrounding the disc flower. The ray florets are involute for ⅔ or more of their length. It is the only dahlia form in which the color classification is determined by the reverse color of the ray floret.

The orchid originated in the early 1900s. France and Germany were the first countries to grow it. It has been called orchis, stella, clematis, star, and orchid-flowered. The ADS first listed the orchid in 1949.

The orchid is valued for artistic floral designs, bouquets, and arrangements. The photos in this section of the chapter represent eight color classes.

670 Seedling (CO LB W/L/w, McClaren, USA) is pastel lavender blending to a white edge on well-formed petals in a flat plane. It grows on a tall healthy plant with many blooms on strong straight stems. Good substance makes it a cut and show flower. Wins its Class. McClaren

673 'Show Off' (CO DB PR/W/w, Swan Island Dahlias, 1999, USA) is purple blending to white outlining the petals, with evenly spaced white petaloids—very attractive, it is aptly named. Grows on a healthy floriferous plant. Wins its Class. Swan Island Dahlias

672 'Jack O Lantern' (CO FL/OR/Y/v/or/y, Swan Island Dahlias, 1989, USA), a flame of bright orange blending with a bright yellow, has evenly spaced petals of different shapes with twisted points and notched tips; the petaloids have the same flame colors. It is easy to grow on fully branched plants. Wins its Class. S. McClaren

674 'Cher Ami' (CO V/OR/Y/v/y/or/w, Larkin/Zydner, 2000, USA) is yellow with orange markings on round evenly spaced petals; the petaloids have orange and white markings on yellow and are ½ the length of the petals. Many early dainty blooms grow on a healthy 18 in. (45 cm) plant. Wins its Class, Best Single and Triple Collarette in Show, and Cream of the Crop. McClaren

ORCHID PHOTOS

741 'Alpen Snowbird' (O W/w, McClaren, 2003, USA). Evie Gullikson Award (trial gardens). This orchid is white with a clean white reverse. The ray florets are evenly spaced and straight, involute for ⅔ their length and touching for ⅓ on a flat plane. Many perfect large 5 in. (12.5 cm) blooms are carried on a tall fully branched plant on sturdy straight stems. Produces an abundance of large tubers that keep well in storage. An easy flower to grow in all climates. Tolerates heat. McClaren

741 Seedling (O W/db/r/y, McClaren, USA) is a striking white on the reverse and blends of red and yellow on the face, with blunt petals in a flat plane. Many blooms are borne on a medium plant. Wins its Class. McClaren

742 'Golden Star' (O Y, L. Connell, 1981, USA) is a bright yellow with tightly rolled petals that are often out of plane. An easy plant to grow, with many early blooms. Wins its Class, Best Single and Triple Orchid in Show, and Cream of the Crop. ADS slide library

742 Seedling (O Y, McClaren, USA) is bright yellow with blunt petals in a flat plane. Blooms of firm substance appear on strong straight stems on a healthy plant early in the season. Wins its Class. McClaren

743 'K-K-K-Katie' (OR/or, Van Dyke, 1996, USA) is bright red-orange on the reverse and face of the ray florets. Petals are unevenly spaced and involute for less than ⅔ of their length. Easy to grow on a healthy plant with many early blooms and good tuber production. Wins its Class, Best Single Orchid in Show, Cream of the Crop, and Fabulous Fifty. McClaren

745 'Lupin Shiela' (O DP/w, Morin, 2000, USA). Derrill W. Hart and Lynn B. Dudley awards. This is a perfect orchid with blunt petals evenly spaced and in a flat plane. Easy to grow in all climates and tolerates heat. Wins its Class, Best Single and Multiple Orchid in Show, Cream of the Crop, and Fabulous Fifty. McClaren

746 'Alpen Rocket' (O R/y, McClaren, 2002, USA) is bright nonfading red on the reverse and yellow on the face of the ray floret. Evenly spaced petals in a flat plane are involute for ⅔ and touching for ⅓ of their length. Easy to grow in all areas on a healthy fully branched plant with an abundance of early blooms and good tuber production; tubers keep well in storage. Wins its Class and Best Single and Triple Orchid in Show. McClaren

753 'Amy's Star' (O DB W/PR/db/pr/y, Rissetto, 1998, USA). Lynn B. Dudley Award. This perfectly formed orchid is a dark blend of white and purple on the reverse and dark blend of purple and yellow on the face of the ray floret. Petals are evenly spaced, blunt, and in a flat plane. Easy to grow on a tall healthy fully branched plant with many early blooms and an abundance of tubers that keep well in storage. Wins its Class, Best Single and Multiple Orchid Bloom in Show, and Cream of the Crop. McClaren

753 Seedling (O DB R/W/r/w, McClaren, USA) is red blending to white on the reverse and red blending to white on the face with well-formed petals in a flat plane. It is easy to grow and wins its Class. McClaren

755 Seedling (O BI DR/W/db/dr/w, McClaren, USA) is dark red with white tips on the reverse and a dark blend of dark red and white on the face of the petal. It is a perfect orchid, with petals tightly rolled. Easy to grow with many tubers, and needed in its class. McClaren

747 'Alpen Sami' (O DR lb/w/r, McClaren, 2003, USA) is dark red on the reverse and light blend of red and white on the face of the ray floret, which is involute for ⅔ and touching for ⅓ of its length. Large 5 in. (12.5 cm) blooms are easy to grow on a fully branched plant with many early blooms and an abundance of tubers that keep well in storage. Wins its Class and Best Single and Multiple Orchid in Show. McClaren

PEONY PHOTOS

PEONY

The peony dahlia is an open-centered flower with two or more rows of ray florets surrounding the disc flower.

Early dahlias were often named after a flower with a similar form. The original peony dahlia was a fully double flower similar in form to the herbaceous peony. The names used for the peony over the years include charm, rosette, paeony-flowered, and peony-flowered. Several early varieties had dark foliage that can still be seen in some peony varieties. Early in the 1920s the ADS classified the peony.

Newer peony introductions are smaller in size than those being shown in the 1970s; many are the smallest dahlias grown. Plant heights vary from 8 to 24 in. (20 to 60 cm); plants are useful as borders and potted plants. The photos in this section of the chapter represent nine color classes.

623 'Brenda Sue' (PE OR, Ellison, 2000, USA) has perfect form and heavily cupped bright petals that are progressively smaller toward the disc. It is easy to grow on a small healthy plant with many petite blooms. Wins its Class, Best Single and Triple Peony in Show, Cream of the Crop, and Fabulous Fifty. S. McClaren

625 'Elvira' (PE DP, Eckhoff, 1994*, USA) is purplish dark pink with perfect form. It grows on a small healthy plant with many early blooms. Wins its Class, Best Single and Triple Peony in Show, and Cream of the Crop. McClaren

621 'Miss Muffit' (PE W, 1981*) is a clean white with perfect form and more than two rows of petals that are progressively smaller toward the disc. It is easy to grow on a small healthy plant with many petite blooms on sturdy stems. Wins its Class, Best Single and Triple Peony in Show, and Cream of the Crop. S. McClaren

624 'Powder Gull' (PE PK, Gullikson, 1995, USA). Lynn B. Dudley Award. This perfectly formed peony is a soft pastel pink, with petals progressively smaller toward the disc. It is easy to grow on a short healthy plant with many early blooms on sturdy stems. Wins Best Single and Triple Peony in Show, Best Basket in Show, Best Potted Plant in Show, Cream of the Crop, and Fabulous Fifty. McClaren

626 'Japanese Bishop' (PE R, 1960*) is orange-red with deep mahogany foliage. It is easy to grow on a healthy low-growing plant with excellent tuber production; tubers keep well in storage. Wins its Class, Best Single and Triple Peony in Show, and Cream of the Crop. Alan Fisher

627 'Bishop of Llandaff' (PE DR, Treseder, 1927, UK), one of the oldest dahlias still being grown and shown and often the jewel of the garden, is bright-dark nonfading red with glossy dark mahogany foliage. The bloom tends to be out of plane with uneven petal placement. Wins its Class, Best Peony in Show, and Cream of the Crop.
Allan M. Armitage

628 Seedling (PE L, McClaren, USA), a dark lavender with excellent form, is borne on a healthy bushy plant with many blooms on straight stems. Easy to grow and needed in its class. Wins its Class and Best Peony in Show. McClaren

629 Seedling (PE PR, McClaren, USA) is clean purple with well-placed petals. It is easy to grow on a small healthy plant with many early blooms, all the same medium size and shape—easy to match for collections. Wins its Class and Best Single and Triple in Show. McClaren

630 'Tinker Bell' (PE LB/W/Y, Holm, 1982, USA), a light blend of white with a yellow eye-zone and a reverse of pastel lavender, has perfect form with involute petals. It is easy to grow on a healthy plant with many small blooms and excellent tuber production; tubers keep well in storage. Wins its Class, Best Single and Triple Peony in Show, and Cream of the Crop. McClaren

ANEMONE

The anemone dahlia has one or more rows of ray florets surrounding a center of elongated tubular disc flowers.

The form dates back to the 1800s, when the anemone was hybridized in Ireland and Germany. Few varieties were known until well into the 1900s, when they were reported in Europe. The ADS classified anemones in the early 1920s. They have also been known as globe and hollyhock dahlias. 'Comet', introduced in Holland in 1952, was the most noted anemone until the late 1990s.

Twentieth-century literature held that the anemone flower was sterile and would not produce offspring. But Evie Gullikson, a hybridizer from Washington State, furnished seed from her crosses and shared them with anyone in the world interested in growing anemones. In 1998 she introduced 'Goldie Gull', now the most popular anemone grown. Evie Gullikson has since passed away, but the seed and their offspring are being grown in countries throughout the world, and many new anemones are being introduced.

The anemone is often used in Japanese floral designs, artistic designs, and bouquets. The unique form makes it easy to distinguish from all other dahlia forms. The disc flower can have one of two petal shapes, either tubular or carnation form. The photos in this section of the chapter represent seven color classes.

ANEMONE PHOTOS

642 'Lucky Ducky' (AN Y/y, Swan Island Dahlias, 2003, USA) has pastel yellow ray florets, sometimes out of plane, and bright yellow pincushion disc flowers. It grows on a healthy plant. Good substance and strong stems make it a valuable cut and show flower.
Swan Island Dahlias

642 'Powder Puff Polka' (AN Y/y, 2002*) has yellow blends of cupped, evenly arranged ray florets visible from the face of the bloom; the disc flowers are yellow, a mixture of tubular and split petals, with a domed pincushion effect. Wins its Class and Best Single Anemone in Show.
S. McClaren

642 Seedling (AN Y/y, McClaren, USA) has pastel yellow evenly spaced ray florets visible from its face; the disc flowers are tubular in shape, forming a perfect yellow pincushion. It is easy to grow on a tall healthy plant with many blooms held on tall straight stems. Wins its Class and Best Single and Triple Anemone in Show. McClaren

646 'Alpen Fury' (AN R/fl/y/r, McClaren, 1995, USA) has red evenly spaced round-tipped ray florets that cannot be seen from the face; the disc flowers, a flame blend of red and yellow, are made up of tubular and split petals with an excellent pincushion effect. Easy to grow on a healthy plant with many blooms with long stems. Produces an abundance of tubers that keep well in storage. Wins its Class, Best Single and Triple Anemone in Show, Cream of the Crop, and Fabulous Fifty. McClaren

646 'Parkland Goldilocks' (AN R/r/y, Rowse, 1999, USA) has red evenly spaced round-tipped ray florets that are not clearly visible from the face; the disc flowers are red with tips of gold, a well-formed domed pincushion. Easy to grow on a healthy fully branched plant with many small early blooms. It has excellent tuber production; tubers keep well in storage. Prefers some shade for best color. Wins its Class. McClaren

647 'Alpen Embers' (AN DR/fl/r/y, McClaren, 1994, USA) has a single row of dark red round-tipped ray florets, evenly spaced, that can be viewed from the face of the bloom; the tubular disc flowers are dark red with yellow tips and unevenly spaced, giving a weak pincushion effect. Easy to grow on tall fully branched plant with many flowers. Prefers a cool climate for good blooms. Wins its Class. McClaren

647 'Alpen Glitter' (AN DR/fl/r/y, McClaren, 2004, USA) has dark red evenly spaced ray florets visible from the face; the disc flowers are dark red with yellow tips and tubular, forming a full pincushion. It grows on a tall healthy plant with many blooms held on strong straight stems. Wins its Class and Best Single and Triple Anemone in Show. McClaren

647 Seedling (AN DR/dr/y, McClaren, USA) has dark red, nearly black, ray florets, not all in a plane, and a well-defined pincushion of tubular disc flowers, dark red with golden tips. Grows on a short plant with early blooms. Wins its Class. McClaren

648 'Alpen Pearl' (AN L/lb/w/y, McClaren, 1997, USA), originally classified as a light blend and changed in 2003 to lavender, has pale lavender ray florets with disc flowers a light blend of white and yellow. It is easy to grow on a healthy plant with many blooms and produces an abundance of tubers that store well. Wins its Class, Best Single and Triple Anemone in Show, and Cream of the Crop. Alan Fisher

649 'Que Sera' (AN PR/pr/y) has purple ray florets with purple and yellow disc flowers. A perfect anemone: the ray florets show, and the disc has great pincushion form. Should win its Class and higher awards when available. Alan Fisher

649 Seedling (AN PR/db/pr/y, McClaren) has evenly spaced round-tipped pleated ray florets in shades of deep purple, which can be viewed from the face, and perfect tubular disc flowers, in dark blends of royal purple with golden tips, forming a domed pincushion effect. Easy to grow on a short plant, with blooms of firm substance carried on well-proportioned stems. Wins its Class, Best Single and Triple Anemone in Show. McClaren

NOVELTY OPEN PHOTOS

650 'Goldie Gull' (AN LB/Y/PK/y, Gullikson, 1998, USA) is a light blend of yellow and pink with several rows of evenly spaced round-tipped ray florets, which can be viewed from the face of the bloom, and yellow tubular disc flowers in a perfect domed pincushion. Easy to grow on a very tall healthy plant with great stems and many perfect large blooms. Wins its Class, Best Single and Triple Anemone in Show, Cream of the Crop, and Fabulous Fifty. McClaren

651 'Scarabella' (AN BR/db/br/y, 1991*) has reddish bronze involute pointed ray florets, evenly spaced and easily viewed from the face; the tubular disc flowers are dark bronze with yellow tips, perfectly formed. Stock is difficult to locate. Wins its Class, Best Single and Triple Anemone in Show. McClaren

NOVELTY OPEN

The novelty open dahlia is an open-centered flower that possesses characteristics different and distinct from other open-centered dahlia forms.

The novelty open, first listed in 2002, is one of the newest classes for the ADS and has the smallest number of varieties (the ADS introduced the novelty class in 1984, which included both the double and open-centered flowers). Now that the novelty open dahlia is judged separately from the novelty fully double, there is renewed interest in this form. The photos in this section of the chapter represent four color classes.

761 'Parkland Seedling' (NO W/dr/w, Rowse) has a white reverse, dark red ray florets with blunt petals, and white finely laced petaloids. Jim Rowse

765 'Alpen Blush' (NO DB DP/w/w, McClaren, 1992, USA) is dark pink and white blend on the reverse with white ray florets and white petaloids. Tends to be out of plane. Wins its Class, Best Single and Triple Novelty Open.
ADS slide library

767 'Alpen Pops' (NO DR/dr, McClaren, 2003, USA) has dark red, nearly black, ray florets and dark red disc flowers. The many disc petals are fully notched and not tubular, and their full petalage makes the ray florets invisible from the face. Many early blooms are carried on well-proportioned stems on a healthy low-growing plant. Easy to grow and produces an abundance of large tubers that keep well in storage. Wins its Class. McClaren

774 Seedling (NO V L/DR/v/l/w/dr, McClaren, USA) is lavender with dark red markings and petaloids of lavender with dark red and white markings. With its unique coloring and nearly double rows of petals, it is needed in its class. An arranger's delight. McClaren

CHAPTER 8

Propagation and Cultivation of Dahlias

PROPAGATION

Once the decision has been made to grow dahlias the choices of propagation are the same regardless of the grower's location, climate, or soil conditions: plant tubers or seeds, or take cuttings. Planting tubers or rooted cuttings will produce offspring identical to that of the parent plant. Planting seeds will produce offspring different from the parent plants but with some characteristics of both the seed parent and the pollen parent.

Tubers

A lifetime of growing dahlias often begins when gardeners are given dahlia tubers by a neighbor or friend. Tubers are underground stems that are modified for food storage and grow in clumps. Each clump has a varying number of tubers. Individual tubers are obtained from these clumps.

Pot tubers are grown from a rooted cutting, either stem or leaf. Each is transplanted into a 4 to 6 in. (10 to 15 cm) pot, and they are grown in the garden, in pots, until they bloom. Remove the pots from the ground, remove the tops, and store the tubers in the pot in a cool location. In the spring the tubers are removed from the pots and used for stem cuttings or divided and used as regular tubers. Pot tubers store well for long periods and make many stem cuttings. Dahlias that do not keep well can be grown successfully from pot tubers.

Cuttings

Cuttings are an economical and efficient way to increase stock of a particular variety. There are two sources from which to get plant cuttings. One is from the tuber and the other is from the plant stalk.

Cuttings from tubers, or stem cuttings, make it possible to grow a number of plants from one tuber. Stem cuttings can be started in a greenhouse, cold frame, basement, garage, or even in the garden. No matter what location is used the cutting process is always the same.

A basement with cool-white fluorescent lighting is a satisfactory location to start cuttings. First, design and build a cutting bench. Cutting benches may vary in size depending on the number of tubers used for cuttings. An ideal cutting bench is 36 in. (90 cm) long by 24 in. (60 cm) wide by 4 in. (10 cm) deep.

Dahlia clump. Photo by McClaren.

Dahlia tuber. Photo by McClaren.

Covered and labeled tuber on the cutting bench, with eye exposed. Photo by McClaren.

Cover the bottom of the cutting bench with 1 to 2 in. (2.5 to 5 cm) of sterile damp potting medium. In February or March, remove the tubers needed for cuttings from the storage area. Place the tubers horizontally in the cutting bench and cover with damp medium, while leaving the eye of the tuber exposed. Label the tuber for easy identification. Soil temperature should be 70 to 80°F (21 to 27°C) for optimum growth.

In two to three weeks the cutting should be ready to be taken from the tuber. Cuttings can be removed when the growth has reached 1 in. (2.5 cm) or longer. To remove the cutting, cut the stem ⅛ in. (0.3 cm) from the tuber using a razor blade or a snap blade knife. Cutting too close to the tuber may damage the eye and stop future stem growth. In one or two weeks another cutting will be ready to take. Continue taking cuttings from the tuber as long as it produces, or until you have the number of cuttings needed. Dip the tip of the cutting in a rooting hormone. Place the cutting in a small pot

Cutting in small pot with potting soil.
Photo by McClaren.

1 WEEK   **2 WEEKS**   **3 WEEKS**

Growth of dahlia cuttings over three weeks. Photo by McClaren.

filled with damp, sterile potting soil, or in damp rooting cubes. Keep the cuttings in a humid environment for two to three weeks or until well rooted. Cuttings develop rapidly during the first several weeks. During this time, it may be necessary to artificially increase the humidity by misting. If using rooting cubes, transplant to small pots when the cuttings are rooted. Once cuttings develop roots, do not overwater, or roots will rot due to inadequate oxygen.

It is important to harden-off the cuttings before transplanting them to the garden. This is done by moving the plants outdoors to a shaded protected area, allowing the plant to acclimate to outdoor weather prior to transplanting to the garden. Stem cuttings root easily in spring and early summer, but after midsummer they are very difficult to root unless they are given supplemental lighting to increase the daylength.

Leaf cuttings are the second way to take cuttings and can be taken any time the dahlia plant is growing. Leaf cuttings are taken from the stalk of the dahlia plant and include a pair of leaves, each with an undeveloped node. Cut the stalk ¼ in. (0.6 cm) below the node and ¼ in. (0.6 cm) above the node, leaving the leaves attached. Split the stalk lengthwise to separate the nodes and cut away the major portion of the leaves. Dip the cut portions of the stem in rooting hormone and pot in damp sterile potting soil. As the leaf dries up, the node begins growing, and leaves and stem develop. When the roots are well developed, harden-off the leaf cutting and transplant to the garden. If the leaf cutting is taken in an area with short seasons and is not transplanted to the garden early in the growing season, the plant will not develop tubers before frost. The plant must then be planted in a pot and overwintered in a protected area, such as a greenhouse or under lights, until it is planted the following spring.

One very important and necessary use for leaf cuttings is the propagation of sports. A sport is a flower that, because of a gene mutation, has characteristics different from the rest of the flowers on the same plant. Dahlias have a tendency to produce sports, and many bicolor dahlias have been propagated from sports. Sports often develop in the late summer or fall and can be propagated by a leaf cutting taken from the branch that produced the sport.

Seed

Very few dahlias will grow true from seed; rather, they will have some characteristics of each of the two dahlia parents that produced the seed. Many growers only want to grow varieties that are named and classified, therefore will not attempt to grow dahlias from seed.

For those wanting to experiment with new varieties, growing dahlias from seed is a rewarding experience. For a full explanation of hybridizing dahlias, see chapter 11.

Stalk of plant with undeveloped nodes for leaf cuttings. Photo by McClaren.

Stalk cut ¼ in. (0.6 cm) above and below nodes with leaves attached. Photo by McClaren.

Stalk split with leaves trimmed. Photo by McClaren.

GROWING DAHLIAS ORGANICALLY

Organic methods have been used throughout the history of agriculture, but it was not until 1940 that the word "organic" was adopted for growing plants. Since then, many different people, organizations, states, and governments have attempted to officially define and set standards for the term. In 1990, the U.S. Congress passed the Organic Foods Production Act to establish a national standard for "organic." In 1997, the U.S. Secretary of Agriculture announced the rules for a National Organic Program. At last there was a set of rules governing organic growing, with special requirements denoting "certified organic." Growers can use organic methods and principles without being certified.

When grown organically, tubers have better overall health and complete their storage cycle in excellent shape; the plants do not lose their vigor and have less fungal and bacterial growth.

The garden will have an outbreak of insects the first year when using only organic methods; however, with a little patience, the beneficial predators will eventually get the pest population under control. You must completely change your attitude to use organic methods—which is difficult after many years of attempting to have an insect-free garden using insecticides. But soon your garden is more predator-friendly, a healthier place for animal and human use. Dahlia bouquets are taken to nursing homes and hospitals without concern. Visitors are welcome to the garden without being concerned about spray contamination, and flowers are of show quality. It is less expensive and less labor-intensive to use organic gardening methods.

Growing organically adds to the overall enjoyment and satisfaction of gardening and contributes to the health and well-being of families, friends, the earth, and the world. As far as growing dahlias, organic growing practices concern four areas: soil, fertilizers, water, and insects.

Dahlia growers often notice that dahlias lose vigor and health after using all the recommended applications of the latest insecticides and chemical fertilizers. Soil can become difficult to plant and till. It seems dead, lacks humus and living organisms. The tubers become less healthy and do not keep satisfactorily in storage. It is time to improve the health of the soil by organic methods.

Commercial companies that carry products that will assist you in growing organically are listed in appendix 1. Since humidity, weather, temperature, and growing conditions differ it will be necessary to determine which organic methods and controls are best for your area.

Soil

Soil can be defined as the uppermost stratum of the earth's crust, which has been modified by weathering and organic activity. The condition of the soil is the most important aspect of growing dahlias organically.

There are three basic soil textures, classified by the size of the soil particles: sand, silt, and clay. The soil's ability to hold water and nutrients corresponds to the size of the soil particles. The pH of the soil is another important characteristic of the soil because it affects the availability and solubility of plant nutrients. Adjusting soil pH is discussed in greater detail in the next section, "Fertilizers."

Healthy soils contain humus, which is decomposed and partially decomposed plant material, and soil microorganisms, such as bacteria and fungi, that are responsible for the decomposition process. Leaves, compost, straw, or grass clippings should be added to the garden yearly, or more often, to resupply the source of organic plant material needed to make humus.

Planting a cover or "green manure" crop is another way to add organic matter to the soil. Generally, a cover crop is any crop grown to provide soil cover. Organic growers are interested in cover crops that are tilled under to produce humus and nutrients for the soil. Organic material that produces humus can be grown from many crops such as buckwheat, oats, rye, and winter wheat. Cover crops of legumes such as alfalfa, clovers, soybeans, peas, and fava beans not only add humus to the soil but also fix atmospheric nitrogen into a form plants and microorganisms can use. Because legume cover crops add nitrogen to the soil, they are often referred to as "green manure" crops.

There are two important things to keep in mind when planting cover crops. First, when planting any of the legumes just listed, make sure the seed has been inoculated with the correct nitrogen-fixing bacteria or the cover crop may grow poorly, or not at all. Second, till under the cover crop before it goes to seed or the cover crop itself may become a weed in your dahlia garden.

If you have adequate garden space it is advisable to plant dahlias in a different area each year and rotate dahlia crops with one of the cover crops. This plan is not practical for most dahlia growers but, with a little ingenuity, the end result can be the same. Use the following method to add organic material to the garden. During the early summer months, grow buckwheat between the dahlia rows, and, four to six weeks after planting, till it under. Next, plant a late cover crop of clover, leave it in the ground over winter, and then till it under in early spring. In cold climates, tops of the dahlia plants are removed and placed on the cover crop, preparing the garden for winter protection. In the following season, plant in the last year's rows and plant cover crops where the dahlias grew.

When planning an organic dahlia garden, the main goal should be to find a way to maintain healthy soil, rich in humus and microorganisms. With experimentation find the method that is the most satisfactory in your area, and increase your soil's productivity from year to year.

Cover crop of buckwheat and dahlia rows. Photo by McClaren.

Cover crop of clover. Photo by McClaren.

Fertilizers

Dahlias need a well-rounded fertilizer program, including nitrogen for good growth, phosphorus for plant maturity and the development of flowers, and potassium for root formation and increased disease resistance. The addition of humus and organic material increases trace elements, microorganisms, and furnishes food for the earthworms.

When the soil is heavy and alkaline, add garden sulfur in the spring to lower the pH and gypsum to aerate the soil; in many areas, soils are acid and need to have lime added. To determine the soil pH take or secure a soil test. Sandy soils need humus added yearly to increase water

Garden ready for winter. Photo by McClaren.

retention. In the spring, add organic material such as leaves and compost; this is tilled in with the cover crop of clover, which adds humus as well as nutrients. There are many ways to make compost; all seem equally successful for an all-around fertilizer. Early in the season an organic foliar fertilizer can be used on the young plants. Repeat the fertilizer program each year, and grow healthy dahlias throughout the growing season. Tubers grown in organic soil store well for long periods.

For those lacking space or unable to use cover crops there are many commercial organic fertilizers that work satisfactorily and keep the soil healthy. See under "Organic Gardening Supplies" in appendix 1 for more information.

Water

Water is the important ingredient that connects soil and fertilizer. It is the dispersant that delivers the nutrients to the roots. Dahlias need an abundance of water throughout the growing period. Their feeder roots are shallow and require moisture at all times. It is necessary for roots to have oxygen to grow successfully. This is possible when the soil is sandy or adequate organic material is present in the soil to produce air pockets. All soils that have poor drainage or clay soils with very fine particles lack space for oxygen. Dahlias can have well-balanced soils and proper fertilizers, but overwatering will destroy the plant by depriving the tubers of adequate aeration.

Dahlias need at least 1 in. (2.5 cm) of moisture per week. If it is not furnished by rainfall then it must be supplemented by other sources of water such as misting, drip, or flooding. In areas of low humidity it is useful to water from overhead risers so that the plants have plenty of moisture above and below the ground. When growing large flowers for the show table a second source of water may be needed so the flowers do not become saturated with water, which causes the stems to break. In areas of low humidity, give the dahlias 10 to 20 minutes of overhead watering daily whenever the temperature rises above 90°F (31°C). This has a cooling effect and raises the humidity, helping to avoid stress on the plants.

Insects

Insects are the largest group of organisms on the earth. There are over 700,000 species of insects, which is more than any other animal group. Their diversity is as great as their population. They inhabit every area of the earth in all habitats. For the past century man has attempted to destroy all those insects that are destructive to plant life without success. As the poisons become more potent the insects are able to evolve and become resistant.

The insect world is made up of three types: beneficials that eat other insects, pests that eat plants, and those that survive on both plants and insects. For the perfect balance in nature, all three kinds are necessary. The difficulty with poisons is that they kill all insects, both pests and beneficials. Once a spray program begins it must be continued on a regular basis since all beneficials have been destroyed and no longer offer protection. It is time to try to control the damage done by spraying, it is time to use less harmful methods.

Private property can be certified as backyard habitat. The habitat elements are food, cover, water, and places to raise young. This habitat encourages an abundance of birds, all insects, and wildlife. All areas have many native beneficials, such as lady beetles, lacewings, pirate bugs, and predators for thrip and mites; dahlia stalks are used during the winter to cover the soil to protect predators. The use of yellow and blue organic sticky strips helps identify and assist in identifying garden insects. With the proper balance of insects the predators will control the pests. Overhead watering assists in controlling many pests, especially mites, which cannot tolerate high humidity.

DAHLIA DISEASES

There are four main causes of diseases in dahlias: environmental, fungal, bacterial, and viral. An unfavorable environment causes the following problems: malnutrition, improper balance of elements, extreme acidity or alkalinity, improper amounts of water. More recent problems have been caused by herbicides coming into contact with the soil, water, plants, mulch, and organic material used in the garden. Dahlias are very susceptible to herbicides in all forms. Any of the problems just listed have a similar effect on the plants, with similar symptoms. The growth is retarded, with yellowish, weak, and sickly foliage, and the root system is poorly developed. To correct the condition the environment must be changed. It takes thorough investigation of the foliage and plant to recognize the cause of the problem.

Fungi and bacteria can cause diseases. Fungi usually travel by spores in the air and spread from plant to plant. Bacteria do not produce spores so must be spread by other means, such as water, garden tools, or insects. Fungi spread much more rapidly than bacteria. Symptoms of fungi on dahlias are sickly foliage with grayish, black, or brown spots. To control fungi growths, use organic fungicides, water early in the morning, keep the garden free of fungal materials such as dying and diseased plants, and remove the lower set of leaves of each plant. Fungal growth may be avoided by using organic practices.

One of the few diseases on dahlias caused by bacteria is crown gall. This is a rough-gall tumor caused by bacteria entering through a cut or break on the tuber. The gall develops on the tuber during the growing cycle. It begins as a very small nodule and grows to a large growth by the end of the season. To control, remove the infected plant from the garden and destroy; using the infected tubers as planting stock spreads the bacteria. Bacterial growth too may be avoided by gardening organically.

Dahlia growers fear viral diseases especially. Several virus types affect dahlias, each with different characteristics. Nearly all viruses cause a yellowing along the veins of the leaf and often stunt the plant. There is no known cure, so obviously virused plants should be destroyed. Insects often carry viruses from weeds and other plants. One needs to become knowledgeable as to the visual characteristics so diseased plants can be destroyed. Viruses are carried in the plant and tuber. The ADS has an ongoing virus research project at Washington State University in Pullman; it is hoped that, as the research progresses, many unanswered questions will be answered.

Weak yellowish leaf caused by an unfavorable environment. Photo by McClaren.

Leaf with fungus. Photo by McClaren.

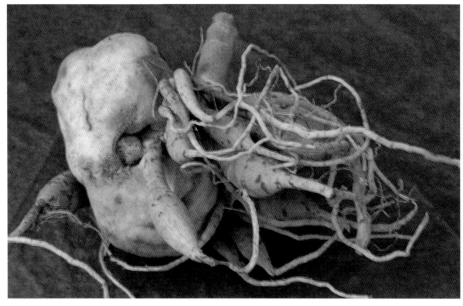

Leaf with virus showing pronounced yellowing along the veins. Photo by McClaren.

Crown gall growing on tuber. Photo by McClaren.

Leaf with virus. Photo by McClaren.

The distance between plants can vary, depending on the size of the plant, from 1 to 3 ft. (0.3 to 0.9 m), and the distance between rows from 3 to 4 ft. (0.9 to 1.2 m) apart. Rooted cuttings should be hardened-off before planting outside. There is less shock to the plant if they can be set out during a cloudy day or protected from the sun by a shade cover for several days. Additional moisture must be furnished until plants are well established.

Dahlia plants with large blooms in areas with wind will need to be staked and tied. Shorter plants with smaller flowers often do not need staking. Many growers will set a 4 to 5 ft. (1.2 to 1.5 m) stake of bamboo, wood, or metal before planting. When the plant reaches a height of approximately 1 ft. (0.3 m), it is tied to the stake. Additional ties will need to be made every 12 to 18 in. (30 to 40 cm), depending on the height of the plant and velocity of the wind.

Weed control is very important since dahlias do not like to compete for nutrients and water. Weeds are also carriers of viruses. Cover crops efficiently control weeds by shutting out sunlight. The feeder roots of dahlias are shallow, so avoid deep cultivation. Hand weeding and mulch are helpful in controlling weeds and conserving moisture.

Topping, disbudding, and disbranching are important summer activities in the dahlia garden. When the plant has three to five sets of leaves, the top growth can be

CARE OF THE DAHLIA GARDEN

Many myths perpetuated by dahlia literature and growers can lead to poor growing practices. Rapidly evolving technology means our agricultural practices are constantly improving, and these changes affect dahlia growers throughout the world. It is important to study the current literature for the latest research on dahlia growing.

Many dahlia growers will plant their tubers and thoroughly enjoy their flowers without a great deal of time spent in the garden. Others find it more satisfying to constantly work with the dahlias trying to improve the plant and flowers. Some of the following practices will give great satisfaction to all dahlia growers.

Dahlias can be planted in rows, in clusters, or singly. In rows they can be planted by size, form, or color, or randomly mixed.

removed to force more branching and flowers. Some dahlia growers remove the side branches of the plants with large flowers. This will limit the number of blooms per plant, increasing the size of the bloom. Disbranching is not necessary for most dahlias; it is used mainly by dahlia specialists for show flowers. The terminal growth of the plant has a large center bud, a side bud, and a growth bud; the side bud and the growth bud should be removed. This is often a difficult thing for beginning dahlia growers to do, but it is necessary for strong, straight stems for each flower. The plant will send up more side branches that will produce more flowers. For the true dahlia show enthusiast, shading the dahlia flowers may be necessary; this may be accomplished with umbrellas, shade cloth, or a combination of shade cloth and umbrellas. Shading improves some colors and avoids the fading of others. Remove fading flowers to lengthen the bloom period for your dahlias.

Dahlia garden with stakes in place. Photo by McClaren.

Dahlia plant being topped. Photo by McClaren.

Disbudding the growth bud.
Photo by McClaren.

Disbudded dahlia plant. Photo by McClaren.

An umbrella shades blooms destined for the show table. Photo by McClaren.

Dahlias under shade cloth. Photo by McClaren.

CHAPTER 9

Care of Dahlia Tubers

A MAJOR FACTOR IN GROWING DAHLIAS successfully is the treatment of the tubers. Tubers that are grown, dug, and stored properly will produce healthy, vigorous plants when replanted.

After the dahlia plant has completed its full growth cycle, it goes dormant. In warm climates the dormancy period can be as short as a few months, and tubers may be left in the ground. In areas where the ground freezes the tubers need to be dug and stored. Dahlia growers often find it difficult to keep tubers viable during long storage. Understanding the correct methods of caring for tubers can simplify the task.

PLANTING AND GROWING HEALTHY TUBERS

Dahlias will tolerate a wide range of soil types and pH levels; however, the healthiest tubers are produced when the plants are grown in a nutrient-rich and organically healthy soil. Compost, organic fertilizer, and humus should be added yearly to maintain soil viability and optimize tuber health and production.

In warm, frost-free climates, tubers may be planted at any time of the year. In climates where it freezes, plant tubers after the danger of frost has passed. Place tubers in the ground 1 to 3 ft. (0.3 to 0.9 m) apart, depending on the size of the plant. The space around each plant needs to be adequate for good air circulation; air movement will keep the plant leaves dry, which helps to discourage airborne plant diseases.

Your garden soil type determines the depth to plant the tubers. The depth of the tuber will depend on the soil structure and temperatures. Sandy soil and high temperatures may require depths of 3 to 4 in. (7.5 to 10 cm); heavy soils with low temperatures, depths of 2 to 3 in. (5 to 7.5 cm). Soil temperature needs to be 50 to 80°F (10 to 27°C) in order for the tuber to break its dormancy and begin growing. If the soil temperature is too cold and wet, tubers can disintegrate. If the soil temperature is too warm, the tubers break down and will not grow. Mark your plantings with tags or stakes so they can be easily identified at digging time.

As discussed in chapter 8, dahlias can be propagated from cuttings. The tubers produced from a cutting will keep well in storage, often better than tubers produced by a plant. The number and form of tubers produced from cuttings depends on the method of planting the cuttings. When planted upright, they will seldom produce more than two misshapen tubers with viable eyes. To increase tuber production and improve the form, let the cutting grow to 8 to 10 in. (20 to 25 cm). Lay the plant horizontally in a 3 in. (7.5 cm) trench, and then cover the roots and cutting to the top set of leaves. As the plant grows it will develop three to five perfectly shaped tubers at each node.

A dahlia plant needs a minimum of three months' growth to develop mature

Dahlia tubers grown from cuttings. Photo by McClaren.

tubers. The feeder root system is shallow on the dahlia plant; deep cultivation can cause root damage and should be avoided. During the growing season, a thorough weed-control program is essential. Dahlias also need consistent watering and fertilizing for healthy tuber production. During the bloom season all spent blooms should be removed, which will increase nutrients to the tuber. Several weeks before digging the tubers, discontinue watering and fertilizing so the tuber growth will slow and tubers will begin hardening-off in preparation for harvest.

DIGGING

Dahlia tubers will be destroyed if they are allowed to freeze so in certain areas they will need to be dug each year. In the short days of fall, the plant's flowers will lose their form and have open centers. The plant will develop weak stems and start setting seed. This is an indication the plants are going into dormancy. The tubers can be dug at any time. After frost the eyes will develop on the tubers and make the tubers easier to divide.

If there is a chance the ground will freeze, leave the frosted tops on the plants until they are dug to help protect the soil and tubers from freezing. Before digging the tubers, remove all ties and stakes.

Check the labels on the tags for correct identification. Cut the top growth from the plant leaving 4 to 6 in. (10 to 15 cm) of stem attached to the base of the plant. This short piece of stalk will give you a convenient place to attach identification tags and it will provide a means for handling the dahlia clump. Use a shovel or digging fork to carefully loosen the soil around the tuber clump and then gently lift it from the ground. Always handle dahlia clumps carefully to avoid breaking the fragile necks on the tubers. Finally, wash all soil from the clump, using a forceful spray of water. The force of the spray should be sufficient to remove all the soil from the clump of tubers; however, it should not be so forceful that the thin protective "skin" that covers the outside of the tubers is damaged.

It is important to divide the tuber clumps and get them in storage as soon as possible. In very dry climates, where the humidity is less than 50%, the tubers should be kept moist while you work to divide them. If the humidity is high, the tubers can be allowed to air dry in the shade. Some growers successfully dig and store the tuber clumps without dividing. Many growers dig only what they can divide and store in the same day. Both methods have advantages. If the clumps are not divided until spring, it is easier to see the new growth, which greatly aids in

Tubers after washing and before they are trimmed. Photo by McClaren.

21-00

Trimmed tubers. Photo by McClaren.

division. Undivided clumps require considerably more storage space than clumps that have been divided.

DIVIDING

Dahlia clumps can be divided and separated into individual tubers with knives, long-nosed clippers, saws, or any tool that will remove the tuber from the clump. Tools used for dividing the tuber clump must be sharp in order to make a clean cut. To help prevent injury, wear rubber or latex gloves and work under adequate light. The long-nosed clipper is an especially safe tool.

Before dividing the tubers, remove any damaged tubers, all root hairs, and any tubers smaller than a pencil in diameter. Leave only the trimmed tubers on the clump. When you divide the clump each tuber must have a viable eye. The eyes are located near the stem of the clump. It is necessary to have an eye on each tuber for new growth to develop the following year. For the first cut, divide the clump into two parts. It is now possible to separate each tuber from the divisions, each with a viable eye. Remove as much of the stem as possible from each tuber. It may be necessary to leave two or three tubers attached in order to keep an intact eye.

As soon as the tubers are divided, identify each one somehow (by name, numerically) with a permanent indelible marker. When marking many tubers of one variety, a rubber stamp kit will speed up the process. Some growers dip their tubers in fungicide or a weak bleach solution before storage; however, no research proves the benefit of such a dipping.

STORAGE AREAS AND STORAGE TECHNIQUES

The most important considerations for a good storage area are humidity and temperature. The ideal inside storage area will have 90% humidity and a temperature of 40 to 50°F (4 to 10°C). The goal for all dahlia growers is to have the tubers remain firm and healthy throughout the storage period. Tubers should look the same when

The first cut, eyes on the stem of the clump. Photo by McClaren.

Two divisions. Photo by McClaren.

they are ready to plant as they did when they were dug in the fall. During the storage period it is important to regularly inspect the tubers to determine their condition, and if necessary, take corrective measures. The first inspection should occur within four to five weeks, then every two months until planting time. If you notice during your inspection that the tubers are starting to shrivel, it is an indication that the humidity is too low in the storage area. In this case, increase the humidity by misting the tubers with a fine spray of clean water. Conversely, if the tubers show signs that they are beginning to rot and disintegrate, remove the affected tubers and lower the humidity in the storage area. When mold is seen during the early days of storage, both temperature and humidity should be lowered. To alleviate storage problems, check the temperature and humidity levels frequently, and adjust as necessary.

Any number of frost-free areas can be used successfully as storage spaces for dormant dahlia tubers. A root cellar is an ideal location for long-term storage. The crisper of a refrigerator stores a small number of tubers (an extra refrigerator can store even more!). Tubers can be stored in insulated containers, ice chests, and cardboard boxes in the coldest area in the basement or crawl space. In areas with light frosts, clumps or divisions of tubers may be placed in trenches in the ground with good drainage and covered with dry

Separated tubers. Photo by McClaren.

leaves and straw to avoid frost.

Several mediums work well for tuber storage. The materials are sterile and safe—newspaper, plastic bags with small ventilation air holes, plastic wrap—and are used to wrap individual or several tubers. Some growers use organic materials such as sawdust, peat, cedar and pine chips; it is possible these materials promote fungal infections in the stored tubers. Other growers prefer to store tubers in perlite or vermiculite or some other sterile inorganic material; both perlite and vermiculite contain a fine dust that can be harmful if inhaled.

Dahlia varieties differ in their ability to survive storage. Some tubers have very thin coverings that allow the moisture to evaporate rapidly, causing the tuber to shrivel and die. The tubers of other varieties cannot tolerate dampness or extreme temperature variations without tuber damage. Tubers grown from cuttings or seed are usually very easy to store.

For additional information on storage techniques, contact local growers or members of a dahlia society in your area for advice. As with all aspects of dahlia growing, do not hesitate to experiment. With experimentation and the guidelines outlined above, you should be able to develop the storage techniques that will give you the best results for your local conditions.

Tubers with identification. Photo by McClaren.

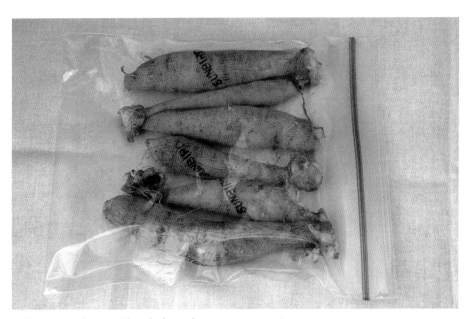

Tubers stored in ventilated plastic bag. Photo by McClaren.

CHAPTER 10

DAHLIA
History and Species

by Marla McClaren

THE DAHLIA FOUND IN A MODERN GARDEN has changed dramatically from the dahlia grown in the gardens of Mexico City over 400 years ago. The first two parts of this chapter review the history of the genus and its species as they made their way from Mexico to the show tables of the modern world; the last concentrates on the species dahlias as parents of the modern dahlia.

"Two species of Acocotli," drawn by Dominguez (Stout 1922).

'Emily D. Renwick', popular cut flower for table decorations (Stout 1922). Photo by McClaren.

HISTORY OF *DAHLIA*

Very little is known about the genus prior to 1570, and although there are reports that the Aztecs used parts of the dahlia plant for food and medicine and its hollow stems for irrigation, little of this can be verified. Following the Spanish Conquest much of the Aztec culture was destroyed, leaving only fragmentary historical records. It is known that Moctezuma maintained a large plant collection at Huaxtepec, and it is possible the dahlia was a part of it.

In 1570 King Phillip II of Spain sent Francisco Hernandez to Mexico to study the natural resources of the country. During his seven years of exploration Hernandez described plants that resemble *Dahlia* species under the names Acocotli and Cocoxochitl. Francisco Dominguez, who accompanied Hernandez, made the first modern drawings of a flower thought to be a dahlia; these were published in 1651. It should be noted, though, that Asteraceae like *Cosmos*, *Bidens*, and *Coreopsis* grow wild in Mexico, and early descrip-

tions do not clearly differentiate these closely related genera.

There are no further reports on the dahlia until 1789, when Vicente Cervantes, director of the Botanical Garden at Mexico City, sent plant parts to Antonio Jose Cavanilles, on staff at the Royal Gardens of Madrid. From these, Cavanilles grew and flowered three new plant forms, which he named *Dahlia pinnata*, *D. rosea*, and *D. coccinea*. Cavanilles named the genus after Andreas Dahl, a Swedish botanist and student of Linnaeus. Pictures of these three dahlias were included in Cavanille's work *Icones et descriptiones plantarum*, published in two parts, in 1791 and 1796. It is interesting to note that one of the plants, *D. pinnata*, is a double-flowered form, and it has since been determined that what was collected and named by Cavanilles as *D. pinnata* was a plant of hybrid origin (Hansen and Hjerting 1996); the wild form of *D. pinnata*, a naturally occurring hybrid, has been renamed *D. sorensenii* (Hansen 1996).

Seed and plant parts from Cavanilles's dahlias were dispersed throughout Europe

beginning in the early 1800s. It was during this period that the scarlet *Dahlia coccinea* was crossed with a mauve-flowered species, possibly *D. pinnata*, resulting in the first modern dahlia hybrids (Lawrence 1929). Growers found the dahlia easy to grow and hybridize, and it quickly became very popular in European and American gardens. Throughout the 1800s and 1900s thousands of new forms were developed; 14,000 cultivars were recognized by 1936 (Sherff and Alexander 1955), and in the past century nearly 50,000 named varieties have been listed in various registers and classification lists. All these forms were hybridized from at least two and possibly all three of the original *Dahlia* species from Mexico. Gerald Weland's extensive review of these individual forms was published in the *Bulletin of the American Dahlia Society* (Weland 1997a).

HISTORY OF THE SPECIES

The genus *Dahlia* consists of 35 species, all of which are found in the highlands of

Mexico and Central America (Sorensen 1969, Saar 2002). Most species have very restricted ranges, and many are probably rare; very few are available to the dahlia grower.

Attempts to describe and categorize the plants in the genus *Dahlia* began soon after they were dispersed in Europe. Between 1804 and 1931 as many as 85 different species were described (Weland 1996); but all this work was accomplished by studying herbarium specimens and plants in cultivation so, in fact, many of the earlier described species were actually garden hybrids.

In the early 1800s the German botanist Willdenow—who was, like most taxonomists of the era, influenced by the groundbreaking work of Carolus Linnaeus—published a classification system using the genus name of *Georgina* instead of *Dahlia* (Willdenow 1810); the mistake was soon realized and the name changed back to *Dahlia*, but georgina is still used as a common name for dahlias in eastern Europe. In 1829 M. Desfontaines suggested that all cultivated dahlias be combined under the species name *Dahlia variabilis*, which binomial, although it is in violation of the International Code of Botanical Nomenclature, is still used in some areas when referring to the garden hybrid. The next year William Smith suggested all dahlias could be divided into two groups, by color: Group I (ivory-magenta) and Group II (yellow-orange-scarlet) (Smith 1830). Many authorities now believe the modern garden dahlia did in fact evolve from hybridization of plants from Smith's two color groups. Giannasi (1975) has studied the pigment in many of the species dahlias and has found that the unique combination of pigments found in *D. coccinea* and *D. sorensenii* match the cultivars, suggesting that these two species may be the parents of the modern dahlia.

The first modern taxonomist to offer a major contribution to the classification of *Dahlia* species was Earl E. Sherff, whose revision of the genus in *North American Flora* suggested 18 species, eight of these previously unreported (Sherff and Alexander 1955).

The next major contributor to the understanding of the genus was Paul D. Sorensen of Northern Illinois University. Sorensen began making trips through Mexico and Central America, collecting herbarium specimens and living plant material, as a graduate student; using field studies, morphological characteristics, and chromosomal studies Sorensen published a revision of the genus *Dahlia* that proposed 27 species, including eight previously unreported (Sorensen 1969). Sorensen continues to the present to publish his work on *Dahlia* species and, with the assistance of his graduate student Dayle Saar, has described three new species.

Dayle Saar is now among the world's leading experts on using molecular techniques to clarify *Dahlia* species. Using DNA sequences to determine ancestral associations as well as field studies, chromosomal analysis, and morphological characteristics, she has proposed a revision to the work done by Sorensen and is continuing her work in molecular analysis of the species dahlias with plans to further depict species relationships.

CURRENT SPECIES OF THE GENUS *DAHLIA* (Saar et al. 2003)

Dahlia apiculata (Sherff) Sorensen
Dahlia atropurpurea Sorensen
Dahlia australis (Sherff) Sorensen
    var. *australis*
    var. *chiapensis* Sorensen
    var. *serratior* (Sherff) Sorensen
Dahlia barkeriae Knowles and Westcott
Dahlia brevis Sorensen
Dahlia campanulata (Saar et al. 2003)
Dahlia coccinea Cavanilles
Dahlia congestifolia Sorensen
Dahlia cordifolia (Sessé and Moc.)
    McVaugh (previously *D. cardiophylla*)
Dahlia cuspidata (Saar et al. 2003)
Dahlia dissecta S. Watson
    var. *dissecta*
    var. *sublignosa* Sorensen
Dahlia excelsa Bentham
Dahlia foeniculifolia Sherff
Dahlia hintonii Sherff
Dahlia hjertingii
Dahlia imperialis Roezl ex Ortgies
Dahlia linearis Sherff
Dahlia macdougallii Sherff

Dahlia merckii Lehman
Dahlia mollis Sorensen
Dahlia moorei Sherff
Dahlia neglecta Saar
Dahlia parvibracteata Saar and Sorensen
Dahlia pteropoda Sherff
Dahlia purpusii Brandg.
Dahlia rudis Sorensen
Dahlia rupicola Sorensen
Dahlia scapigera (A. Dietrich) Knowles
    and Westcott
Dahlia scapigeroides Sherff
Dahlia sherffii Sorensen
Dahlia sorensenii Hansen and Hjerting
Dahlia spectabilis Saar, Sorensen, and
    Hjerting
Dahlia tenuicaulis Sorensen
Dahlia tenuis Robinson and Greenman
Dahlia tubulata Sorensen

Only a few of the 35 recognized *Dahlia* species are available to growers, a situation we can only hope will change in the future. The flowers of most species dahlias have only a single row of petals, so they often get overlooked as garden specimens when compared to their flashier offspring, the hybridized dahlias. In fact many species dahlias are beautiful plants, with qualities that would be of interest to many gardeners, and they possess unique characteristics that make them a valuable asset to hybridization programs; some, for instance, have increased resistance to spider mites and powdery mildew, which strengths would greatly benefit garden dahlias. Most species dahlias are obtained by purchasing seed; true species can be grown from seed and look identical to the parent (whereas plants grown from seed collected from a hybridized dahlia will not look like the parent plant). Most species dahlias with the same number of chromosomes will hybridize with each other and with cultivars, if left to be open-pollinated.

The following are the wild species most readily available to the gardener.

Dahlia coccinea Cavanilles

This species, originally described by Cavanilles from plants he grew from seeds collected in Mexico, is found in a wide range throughout Mexico and Guatemala.

Dahlia coccinea, lemon-yellow form.
Photo by Martin Kral.

Dahlia dissecta, foliage.
Photo by McClaren.

Dahlia coccinea, orange-scarlet form.
Photo by McClaren.

Dahlia dissecta, flowers.
Photo by Ginny Hunt.

Dahlia imperialis, towering over out-
building. Photo by McClaren.

The plant grows 18 to 50 in. (45 to 300 cm) tall with flower color ranging from lemon-yellow to orange, orange-scarlet, and deep blackish scarlet. Ginny Hunt of Seedhunt and J. L. Hudson have offered seed for this plant (see "Sources for Species Dahlias" in appendix 1).

Dahlia dissecta S. Watson

Dahlia dissecta, found on limestone ledges in Mexico, is an herbaceous perennial, growing 12 to 36 in. (30 to 90 cm) high. The leaves are deeply dissected, green with a glossy upper surface. The flower heads, held erect above the foliage, are very pale lavender (almost white) to light purple and 0.8 to 1.6 in. (2 to 4 cm) in diameter. Jim and Jenny Archibald offered

seed for *D. dissecta* in 2000, and Seedhunt plans to offer seed of this species in the near future.

Dahlia imperialis Roezl ex Ortgies

This species is found on rocky slopes and fields at 2500 to 9000 ft. (750 to 2700 m) in Mexico, Guatemala, El Salvador, Costa Rica, and Colombia. This tall plant, some-times called a tree dahlia, can grow to over 20 ft. (6 m) with clusters of beautiful large pendulous lavender single ray flowers hanging near the top of the plant; the white-flowered form, which this author grew, had unimpressive small flowers held erect on 20 ft. (6 m) stems. *Dahlia imperialis* blooms in winter (late November in California) when few other plants are in

bloom. Unfortunately, gardeners with shorter growing seasons cannot appreci-ate the flower. Most of the leaves fall off the lower 10 to 15 ft. (3 to 4.5 cm) of the plant, leaving the lower section looking like a bamboo grove. *Dahlia imperialis* is easily propagated by planting tubers or by trimming its foliage and planting small pieces of stem that contain a node. The plants are sturdy, with large compound leaves; they are at risk of severe wind dam-age and may fare better if planted next to a building or fence so the stalks can be tied to the structure. This species has been offered by Heronswood Nursery.

Dahlia imperialis, foliage.
Photo by McClaren.

Dahlia imperialis, flowers. Photo by McClaren.

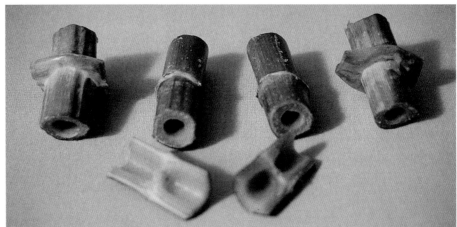

Dahlia imperialis stems with nodes separated for planting. Photo by McClaren.

Dahlia merckii, mixed flower colors. Photo by Ginny Hunt.

Dahlia merckii, floriferous plant.
Photo by Martin Kral.

Dahlia tenuicaulis, foliage.
Photo by McClaren.

Dahlia merckii Lehman

Dahlia merckii is found on rocky slopes in Mexico. It grows 18 to 72 in. (45 to 185 cm) tall with white, lavender, or purple flowers, often as many as 10 to 90 per plant. The plant has vine-like growth and may need to be staked. Several private growers in the United States have stock.

Dahlia tenuicaulis Sorensen

This tree dahlia is found in dense forests of Mexico. It is smaller than *Dahlia imperialis*, growing to about 6 ft. (1.8 m). According to Sorensen (1969), the stems are thinner and the leaves smaller than *D. imperialis*, and it produces fewer flowers. The emerging foliage is red-purple; the dark mauve flowers appear in late summer and early fall (direct communication with Ginny Hunt of Seedhunt). This species was offered by Heronswood Nursery in 2002 and 2003.

CHAPTER 11

Hybridizing and Dahlias of the Future

HYBRIDIZING DAHLIAS

When dahlias are grown from tubers or cuttings, they are a clone of the parent plant. Several varieties, listed in garden seed catalogs, can be grown from seed; most of these are bedding or border dahlias that will be similar to their seed parent. Seedlings grown from hybridized dahlias may have characteristics similar to the parents but will not be identical, and many will not meet present-day standards of dahlias being grown for show. Despite this, growing dahlias from seed can be an exciting and challenging pursuit.

Seed parent (l), seedling (c), and pollen parent (r) showing similar and different characteristics. Photo by McClaren.

Dahlia bud (l) and seedpod (r). Photo by McClaren.

Cross section of bud (l) and seedpod (r). Photo by McClaren.

Dried seedpod labeled. Photo by McClaren.

For those wanting to collect their own seed, the first step is to become acquainted with the difference between the bud and seedpod of the dahlia. The bud is flatter and smaller, and the seedpod is larger and firmer. The bud contains immature flower parts, and the seedpod, mature and immature seed. After the flower blooms and the ray florets fall, the seedpod will have formed. Mark the seedpod, while it is on the plant, with the name of the parent plant and pollen plant, if known. In 10 to 14 days of dry weather the pod is ready to be picked and placed in a dry location. When fully dry, shell out the pod. The seedpod contains mature seed, bracts, immature seed, and dried disc flowers. The mature seeds are firm and full, whereas the immature seeds are small, with only the seed covering, and can be crushed easily between the fingers. The mature seed stays viable for many years if stored in a dry dark location. Use only mature seed for planting. Plant the seed in potting soil and transplant to a 3 in. (7.5 cm) pot when the first set of leaves develops. Grow the plant in a protected area, and plant outside when the danger of frost is past.

Growers often continue to produce seedlings by chance, but it is estimated that if seed is collected randomly from the dahlia patch, only one in a thousand will result in a dahlia that should be saved. There are ways to improve the outcome of dahlia hybridizing, but one needs to be persistent and patient, learning from experience.

Dried seedpod shelled. Photo by McClaren.

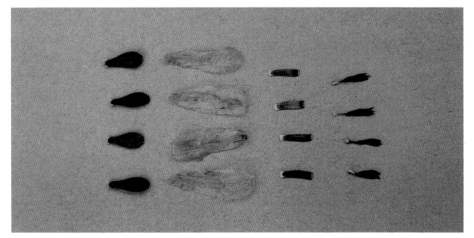

Shelled seedpod composed of mature seed (l), bracts (lc), immature seed (rc), and dried disc flowers (r). Photo by McClaren.

Hybridizing knowledge

The successful hybridizer keeps accurate records of named varieties, documenting their growth habits, strengths, and weaknesses. Having a notepad or a small tape recorder available for notes while in the dahlia garden will help you collect such information. At the end of each growing season summarize the information for the year; this will be invaluable for future reference.

Very few tools are needed for your hybridizing program; these include an official dahlia color chart, the *ADS Classification and Handbook of Dahlias*, and a small measuring tape.

The productive hybridizer has a thorough knowledge and experience of growing, showing, and judging as many forms, sizes, and colors as possible. The best ways to gain knowledge about the dahlia plant are to grow dahlias; join a dahlia society; read dahlia literature; and attend judging schools. The recommended characteristics of form, color, substance, stem, foliage, and bloom position need to be fully understood and easily recognized. Hybridizers need experience in judging first-, second-, and third-year seedlings; undisseminated seedlings; the seedling bench; and the trial garden. Being knowledgeable in judging varieties for other growers is excellent preparation for judging one's own seedlings.

Hybridizing guidelines

Once a hybridizer has become thoroughly knowledgeable by growing and showing named varieties, it is time to develop guidelines for hybridizing seedlings. Many basic guidelines are acquired by the hit-or-miss system of hybridizing, but further information and direction will eliminate the failures and increase the successes.

It is difficult to get predictable results, such as certain colors, forms, or sizes, by selecting random seeds from a garden that has many varieties, which tend to produce seedlings in the middle range and color in the blends. Seed from open-centered flowers grown in a randomly planted garden will develop semi-double and double flowers, which lack petal count. Many seedlings are in classes that already have a large number of flowers. To avoid some of these concerns, a hybridizer should establish a goal for hybridizing.

Start by selecting a favorite form, color, or size of dahlia. This is often a dahlia variety you are familiar with and enjoy growing and showing. Set a goal by determining what you want to accomplish with the dahlia you have chosen. If you truly don't have a favorite dahlia but like all dahlias, choose one anyway. Consider the cases of a few of the most successful hybridizers in the world. In the early 1900s an Australian hybridizer chose to focus on pompons and spent many years of his life improving the pompon form, color, stem, and plant growth; his pompons are still the best and shown throughout the world. Another hybridizer from South Africa has devoted his life to developing B laciniated dahlias. When he started work on the form he was the only grower in the world who thought it had potential; today it is among the most popular dahlias in the world. Others are taking his lead and hybridizing laciniated dahlias of other sizes. Several leading hybridizers in North America and the United Kingdom have spent years hybridizing A and AA sizes. These growers selected one size and form and continued to improve their chosen dahlia throughout their lifetime.

It is difficult to decide what goal will be pursued in the hybridizing program. One way is to study the *ADS Classification and Handbook of Dahlias*, to determine which sizes, forms, and colors are not available; focusing on an area with missing varieties should prove very productive for the beginner. Once you have determined your long-range goal, you are set to begin a challenging experience.

Your goal may be pursued throughout your hybridizing experience, or it may be adjusted after several years. One hybridizer started with the goal of growing early flowering varieties and therefore saved seed from the earliest flowers in the garden. The resulting seedlings, which indeed bloomed several weeks earlier than other dahlias, were in the BB or miniature classes with many blends. The original goal was accomplished, but a new direction was established: to hybridize early dahlias of only miniature cactus.

Once you plant your first seedlings, it is necessary to develop an identification system. Each seedling should be marked with the name of the seed parent and pollen parent if known. Saved seedlings should be assigned the number of the year and the order in which they were saved; for example, the fourth seedling dug and saved in 2003 will be labeled 034. Few first-year seedlings will develop to the point of receiving a unique name; the number is a useful substitute.

This is the start of a successful record system for seedlings. The record system will contain valuable information about the seedling as it is grown and evaluated for its first four years. The information for the first year should include a seedling number, seed and pollen parent, form, color, and any seedling awards. The second year, keep information on color description, bloom size, stem length, height of plant, seedling awards, and the timing of the first bloom (early, medium, or late). In the third year, record tuber health, size, and seedling awards. In the fourth year, record the name, trial garden scores, seedling bench scores, and show awards. Keep general comments each year.

The record keeping may seem excessive, but at the end of each growing season you will need to decide if you will grow the seedling another year. With adequate records a sound decision can be made. Often seedlings are discarded or kept without adequate information. By the time the flower is introduced, you should be thoroughly acquainted with it, and without recording information it is very difficult to remember all the details neces-

Composite flower with ray florets surrounding the disc. Photo by McClaren.

sary to answer questions about the new introduction. The more seedlings you hybridize the more information you need to make sound decisions. Some seedlings are grown and tested for a longer period before sending to trial gardens or bench-tested in open competition with alphanumeric identification.

Hybridizing techniques

Beginning hybridizers will let the flowers set seed and collect the seedpods. Once they start a program with a purpose, however, additional information will be needed and certain questions come to mind. These are the ones I hear most often: how are the seeds formed on a dahlia, how should the plants be isolated and planted, and what plants should be used as seed parents? Many more questions follow.

The dahlia flower is a composite flower made up of ray florets surrounding a disc flower. The ray floret has at the base a stigma that has a divided tip. The disc flower is made up of small tubular disc florets comprised of the male (pollen) and female (stigma) elements of the flower. The disc florets each have a pistil (female) and stamen (male). The pistil is the seed-bearing organ of the flower comprised of the ovary, style, and a stigma that receives

Ray floret with stigma.
Photo by McClaren.

the pollen; the stamen is the flower structure made up of the anther and filament. Pollen, the yellow powder produced by the anthers, functions as the male element in fertilization.

Dahlia plants are typically pollinated by insects. The pollinators most often seen on the flowers are honeybees and bumblebees, but other bees, insects, birds, and wind play an important role in plant pollination. It is rare for dahlias to be self-pollinating, so two varieties are needed for seed production. Since hybridizers select certain parents to cross, they will need to isolate the parent from other dahlias in the garden. The many distances quoted in

Disc florets showing the pistil. Photo by McClaren.

The pistil (seed-bearing organ) comprised of the ovary, style, and stigma. Photo by McClaren.

The pollen from the stamen. Photo by McClaren.

sizes, and colors together in your garden in an isolated area in clusters. This will yield a collection of seeds from similar dahlias; the seedlings will be more predictable than seed collected from a garden planted at random. Another is to plant selected parents in rows; plant one row with plants 1 ft. (0.3 m) apart with another row 1 ft. (0.3 m) away, positioning the plants in the second row so that they are staggered, forming a zigzag pattern, from the first row. By careful placement several different varieties can be arranged so that various combinations are possible, to determine if varieties are compatible. Records will show which plants produce the best seeds and which are successful pollinators. A third way is to plant two different varieties together where each flower can be the seed parent or the pollinator; this will give valuable information about each variety as seed and pollinators.

When you want to know the exact seed and pollen parents, plant in pots that are isolated and hand pollinate. Blooms can also be isolated from pollinators in the garden by covering them with nylon netting or brown paper bags. Hand pollinating is the most successful way of controlling the parentage of seedlings.

The hybridizer will need to know the plant parts to be successful at hand pollinating. A hand lens will assist in seeing the plant parts, and a small paintbrush will be useful in transferring the pollen. In fully double flowers each ray floret has a stigma

dahlia literature, some as far as 100 ft. (30 m), are often unrealistic for the small grower. Insects move from flower to flower and plant to plant—seldom to another row, if the distance is greater than several feet; the distance between parents and other varieties in a row, therefore, does not have to be more than 10 ft. (3 m) for successful controlled pollination. In tests with cactus and orchid dahlias (each with very different ray floret forms), there

was no apparent cross-pollination in the seedlings when planted as close as 8 ft. (2.4 m). If the isolation distance is 10 ft. (3 m), very little cross-contamination by insects will occur. For other sources of pollination such as birds and wind, isolation provided by cover crops and hedges, again at a distance of 10 ft. (3 m), has been used successfully.

There are several ways to plant tubers for pollination. One is to plant like forms,

Hand pollinating a stigma on a ray floret of a double flower. Photo by McClaren.

miniatures produce flowers that are over the required size. Since many of them were hybridized from a larger flower, it may be necessary to introduce genes from a smaller bloom such as the pompon. Once your parent stock has the necessary genes your hybridizing program will progress successfully.

GENETICS OF THE DAHLIA

The genes that have been inherited from the parent plants determine the observable characteristics of a plant. A gene, in the classical sense, is a section of DNA that occupies a specific location on a chromosome and has the ability to affect a characteristic of the plant. Most living organisms obtain one set of chromosomes from each parent, so each cell nucleus contains two genes for any one characteristic. The gene can have a dominant/recessive pattern of expression in which the dominant gene, designated with a capital letter, is expressed despite the presence of a second recessive gene, designated with a lowercase letter.

Gregor Mendel demonstrated purple flower color was dominant to white in the garden pea. This would be denoted as PP for a purple flower with two genes for purple; Pp or pP for a purple flower with one gene for purple and one gene for white (small p is used for the opposite of the dominant gene, which in this case is white); or pp for a white flower with two genes for white. If the genes of the parents are known, the outcome of a cross between these parents can be determined. As an example, the expected outcome of a cross between two plants known to have both the dominant and recessive (Pp) are shown in the table below.

located at the base. As the bloom develops, each row of ray florets will have viable stigmas for approximately one day starting with the outside row of petals progressing to the center of the bloom. The stigma will accept pollen from the anther during midday. Viable stigmas will be shiny and sticky and will accept pollen readily. As the flower matures the disc flower will open in the center of the flower and produce many more stigmas and pollen for viable seeds. Each flower needs to be marked with the seed and pollen plant names. Hand pollination will not produce an abundance of seed but will produce successful seedlings.

As further help to the beginning hybridizer, let's get back to the idea of settling on a goal by using a concrete example. The *ADS Classification and Handbook of Dahlias* shows that the miniature informal decorative dahlias lack many colors. There are no color varieties listed in pink, dark red, lavender, flame, or variegated color classes, and several other colors have only one variety. This would be a form and color that could produce results in several years.

To select seed and pollen parents, the following characteristics need to be examined in the plants of the miniature informal decorative class. The seed parents should have healthy tubers that store well, strong plants with straight stems, early

blooms, and flowers that meet all the required characteristics for the informal decorative form. Select plants that meet these criteria, and plant each in as many combinations as possible in zigzag rows. Keep a map of the order of the plantings. Save the first blooms of each plant. Mark each seedpod with a nametag of the parent plant, year, and the location in the row.

By keeping accurate records for the seedlings from each plant, several hypotheses may be extracted from first-year results. Plants that have produced seed were compatible to the adjoining plant, making them future seed parents. Record which seed parents produce seedlings with the best characteristics of informal decorative form, miniature size, plant health, bloom position, and stem form. All these characteristics often are not achieved the first year and need to be developed before an attempt is made to secure a certain color. Once seedlings are produced with the required characteristics, they will be used as parents to develop the desired color classes.

At this time new genes need to be introduced from flowers that have the requirements to achieve your goal. For the miniature informal decoratives, with so many colors lacking, it may be necessary to use another form of flower, such as a miniature formal decorative or semi-cactus, having the desired colors. Often the

	P	p
P	PP	Pp
p	pP	pp

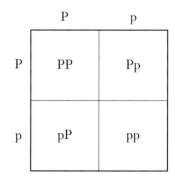

The genes from parent 1 are shown above the grid; those of parent 2 are to the left of the grid; potential offspring are shown in the boxes. There will be one offspring with purple color and two dominant genes; two offspring will have purple color but have one dominant and one recessive gene; and one of the offspring will be white with two recessive genes.

Unfortunately, understanding the inheritance patterns in the dahlia is much more complicated. Each cell of the dahlia plant contains eight sets of eight similar chromosomes (64 chromosomes). Although the eight matching chromosomes are not completely identical, it is possible eight genes instead of two could determine one characteristic. Since Mendel's work with the peas it has been determined that many genes do not express characteristics in a strictly dominant/recessive pattern. Instead, many characteristics of a plant appear to be between the characteristics of the parent plants—for example, a tall plant crossed with a short plant results in a plant of medium height.

Despite the increased complexity of dahlia genetics, certain trends can be noted, and some dahlia hybridizers can hazard generalized predictions concerning the characteristics of dahlia seedlings. One observation is that the seed parent contributes to the seedling's plant health and size and to its tuber health and production, while the pollen parent contributes to the seedling's bloom form. If both parents have the same size and form, the seedling will most likely have that form but the size often is different from that of the parents. Both parents probably determine the petal count; if a ball is crossed with a single, the seedling will have fewer petals than the ball and more than the single. The color often seems to be a combination of the colors of the seed and pollen parents. This has proven to be an accurate assumption since there are many more blends than any solid color, whereas the species are all solid colors. When crossing white with lavender nearly all the seedlings will be a blend of white and lavender. The determining factors of the seedling characteristics need to be constantly examined and researched for more accurate predictions.

Collection of Boley first-year mixed seedlings. Photo by Stephen L. Boley.

SELECTING AND SAVING SEEDLINGS

There are several methods of determining which seedlings should be saved for further consideration. It usually takes a minimum of three years to determine if the seedling has all the necessary characteristics required by the hybridizer and ADS. Space is often a consideration in determining the number of seedlings saved each year. First-year seedlings will produce from one to four tubers, but that may be different the second year. A set of requirements should be established for saving seedlings.

The first-year seedling should have the following characteristics to be saved; all others should be discontinued, which is often the most difficult part of growing seedlings. The form, stem, health of the plant, bloom position, and first-year show results should all be satisfactory. Second-year seedlings are evaluated for tuber health and production, plant size, and second-year show results, in addition to a recheck of first-year requirements. In the third year, the hybridizer's own goals for raising seedlings, such as form, color, plant and tuber health, are considered. In the fourth year, if it has been determined that it is needed in its class, the dahlia seedling should have adequate tubers to be introduced.

Seedlings can also be evaluated by others. Each of these opportunities will help the hybridizer determine if the seedling meets the requirements for each characteristic required by ADS and should be grown another year.

First-year seedlings

The first-year seedling will nearly always bloom the first year. If it does not produce a flower in the first year, the tubers can be planted the next year for a bloom. Each plant will have one to four tubers the first year, with an average of three. If the seedling produces only two tubers it will be nearly impossible to have an adequate number of tubers to introduce it in four years. Many ADS shows have a class for first-year seedlings. Often the first-year seedling is not in bloom at the time it is to be entered in a show. Many hybridizers will wait until the next year before starting to show it as a first-year seedling. If the judges think the dahlia has potential, it will be given a blue ribbon with the recommendation to grow it again.

Second- and third-year seedlings

The next two years the dahlia will continue to be grown and shown in the sec-

First-year seedlings. Photos by McClaren.

Second-year seedlings. Photos by McClaren.

Third-year seedlings. Photos by McClaren.

Collection of Boley second- and third-year pompons. Photo by Stephen L. Boley.

Undisseminated seedling.
Photo by Alan Fisher.

Undisseminated seedling.
Photo by S. McClaren.

ond- and third-year seedling class in open competition, and in special classes. The judging will determine how the flower will compete in its class; the overall flower will be viewed to determine if it should be grown again, and, if so, a blue ribbon is awarded.

Trial gardens and seedling bench trials

When the seedling has been grown for at least four years, it can be shown in the ADS trial gardens, located throughout Canada and the United States, and/or on the seedling bench of an accredited show. The hybridizer sends three tubers or cuttings of the seedling to any number of trial gardens for evaluation. The trial gardens are judged by the required number of certified judges, and those seedlings scoring 85 or above can be introduced and listed in the next *ADS Classification and Handbook of Dahlias*. Each accredited ADS show is required to have a seedling evaluation bench. The seedling is entered with three blooms and scored by a required number of certified ADS judges; if it scores 85 or above it can be introduced.

A seedling that meets the ADS requirements will be ready to introduce. The hybridizer names the seedling, which will need to be different from previously introduced dahlias. At that time ADS will list it in the *ADS Classification and Handbook of Dahlias*. Each country of the world

has different requirements for a dahlia to be a recognized variety, but once a dahlia is recognized in the home country, most other countries will accept it as a named variety.

Undisseminated seedlings

All seedlings that have not been introduced or sold are undisseminated. They are seedlings that have not scored in the trial gardens or on the seedling bench. The hybridizers may lack adequate stock to introduce them even though they are four years old or more.

DAHLIAS OF THE FUTURE

The dahlia, because it is so easy to hybridize, presents endless exciting possibilities—and a promise that the dahlias of the future will be many and varied. Growers throughout the world are hybridizing new dahlias at an unprecedented rate, and interest in dahlias is burgeoning worldwide.

The ADS encourages hybridizers to develop all forms, colors, and sizes. Still there are a number of classes lacking varieties: the AAs lack formal decorative, straight cactus, and incurved cactus, and the miniature class needs informal decorative and laciniated, for instance. The new classes adopted by the ADS in 2002—

Undisseminated seedling.
Photo by McClaren.

novelty fully double, novelty open, and stellar—could stand an influx of all varieties. Several color classes, such as dark pink, purple, variegated, and bicolor, are sparsely represented. More early-blooming varieties are being grown for areas with short growing seasons, and there is renewed interest in dark foliage in all forms of dahlias.

Several new forms are appearing in hybridizers programs. One is the orchid with petaloids, sometimes referred to as the orchette. Another new form is the double flower with petaloids. Open-centered flowers and other forms with laciniated petals are being grown. New petal formations are being hybridized, and there is an interest in the colors green, brown, and black.

With the many new waterlilies, there is interest in creating two size classes (as in the past, the small flower has difficulty competing with the large flower). Short plants with larger flowers are more and more seen; these introductions require less tying and staking in windy areas. By contrast, mignon singles are appearing on tall plants. New seedlings offer many more florets; 'Haystack', a dahlia hybridized by Charles Splinter of California, has over 550 ray florets.

Hybridizers should focus their breeding efforts on creating dahlias that will make great potted plants. Growing areas are becoming limited; more people are living in apartments and smaller dwellings, and often they would like to grow dahlias. To satisfy their needs, smaller plants with petite-sized blooms should be hybridized.

The dahlia of the future will be as varied as the hybridizers' imaginations. Many new hybridizers are bent on creating entirely new dahlia forms; there have been reports of single flowers with eight entirely closed tubular ray florets. At different times in history there have been accounts of fragrance in dahlias, and fragrance has again been reported in 'Hy Scent' (O R/y) and other orchid dahlias. Growers have expressed a strong interest in flowers that are resistant to insects and diseases. If dahlias were less affected by early frosts, gardeners in areas with short seasons would be encouraged to grow more dahlias.

Forty years ago, hybridizers communicated with others only once a year, at a dahlia show; new technology makes it possible for hybridizers throughout the world to keep in close and nearly constant contact. New techniques and ideas are shared by all, in an instant, and new varieties—history has shown us—encourage new growers to join the dahlia world, creating a renewed interest in the genus and its glorious hybrids.

CHAPTER 12

Dahlia Shows, Trial Gardens, and Awards

Upon first seeing a dahlia, people are amazed at their spectacular beauty. The varied sizes, forms, and colors of dahlias lead people to believe they must have been grown in a greenhouse or under other special circumstances. As their interest grows, their hobby becomes a passion, and people seek to share and display their blooms for competition and possible awards, in dahlia shows and trial gardens.

DAHLIA SHOWS

Dahlia shows are held internationally, either separately or as part of a general flower show; they can vary in size from displays of a few to several thousand blooms. The purposes of dahlia shows are varied: to acquaint gardeners and the general populace with dahlias, to educate spectators on the uses of dahlias, to enter seedlings on the seedling bench, and for competition.

Dahlia societies (or circles or clubs, as they are sometimes called) now exist in nearly all countries of the world. Over 70 dahlia societies, all associated with the American Dahlia Society, have been established throughout Canada and the United States; the earliest were founded in the late 1800s. The first dahlia show schedules were often adapted from these local garden clubs.

Judges and clerk at dahlia show.
Photo by McClaren.

Early dahlia shows in the United States were mainly for exhibition; one of the earliest was held in Philadelphia in 1895 (Bailey 1895). By the early 1920s the ADS donated a silver medal to be competed for at any local association show (Stout 1922), and garden clubs were hosting organized dahlia shows that included such classes as cactus, hybrid cactus, decorative, peony-flowered, single or duplex, seedlings, vases, baskets, bouquets, and arrangements. There were three divisions—novice, amateur, and professional—and a great deal of concern regarding the difference between the amateur and the professional. The following rule was adopted by the ADS to clearly define the difference: "An amateur gardener is one who does all the work in the garden except the plowing or spading, and who is not engaged in gardening as a livelihood."

A dahlia's size was paramount at mid-20th-century shows. A great deal of emphasis was placed on the largest flowers in each class, and the ADS often bestowed an award upon the largest flower in the show, a practice which some societies continue even today. Any flower that did not fit the classified size was eliminated from judging. In the late 1980s, however, exact size was no longer emphasized by the ADS as a judgment criterion. Blooms are now placed in their class, listed in the *ADS Classification and Handbook*, and judged by size to a lesser extent. If a variety's size consistently fails to meet its size classification, the flower is recommended for reclassification.

Dahlia shows have in many ways evolved together, with many similarities from one show to the next; however, each society is responsible for the rules and regulations of their individual show. The ADS recommends that each show have classes for all ADS-recognized dahlia classes, and additional classes are often established by the society sponsoring the show. The ADS recommends teams of three judges and a clerk for judging dahlia shows. Results of the society shows are published annually in the *Bulletin of the American Dahlia Society*.

A scale of points or a scorecard can be used to judge each section of a dahlia show. Each show can establish scorecards to meet their show requirements. The following scorecard is given as a guideline for a show schedule.

SINGLES, TRIPLES, AND MULTIPLES SCORECARD	
Characteristics	*Maximum points*
Color	22
Form	28
Substance	15
Stem	10
Foliage	10
Condition	5
Staging and bloom position	
Singles	10
Triples and multiples	5
Uniformity (triples and multiples)	5

The show tables can be arranged with single and triple blooms separated by color class for easier judging. The winners of each section of the show are placed on the awards table.

The height of the entry should be in proportion to the size of the bloom; this is accomplished by disbudding the flower while it is still on the plant. Select blooms for the show with stems in good proportion to the flower.

Show containers can be as varied as the shows. Some shows require all exhibits be displayed in identical containers furnished by the show; this uniformity makes the displays attractive. Other shows require exhibitors to furnish containers; this should be clearly defined in the show

Show table with single mixed flowers.
Photo by Alan Fisher.

Awards table at the conclusion of a show.
Photo by Alan Fisher.

schedule. Triple blooms of the same size and variety are usually exhibited in one container. If exhibitors have a number of blooms of one variety, displays of dahlias can be shown in the multiple bloom class. If multiple bloom classes are of one variety, the size and color need to be uniform. If the schedule stipulates varieties can be mixed, then color and form should be compatible. Some shows have sections of five or more of a kind.

Dahlias can be used in shows in educational ways as well. Classes can be designed to assist spectators in identifying the various forms of dahlias; exhibiting different forms together is a particularly effective way to demonstrate the uniqueness of each. At the ADS National Show in California in 2002, the entrance was

Triple flowers showing desirable uniformity in the field. Photo by Swan Island Dahlias.

Dahlia branch disbudded in preparation for a show. Photo by McClaren.

Flower stem too long for showing. Photo by McClaren.

Triple flowers on the show table. Photo by Alan Fisher.

Flowers on show table in identical containers. Photos by Alan Fisher.

Collection of five or more blooms of a kind. Photo by S. McClaren.

Collection demonstrating distinct forms.
Photo by Alan Fisher.

Large-scale standing arrangement of dahlias and fresh foliage.
Photo by S. McClaren.

The following is a suggested scorecard for baskets:

BASKET SCORECARD	
Quality of blooms	50
Arrangement	15
Color harmony and effect	15
Suitability of container	10
Distinction	10

Baskets are displayed in different ways. One type of basket display incorporates only dahlias and filler (fresh foliage) and is viewed and judged only from the front. Small open-centered dahlias make attractive baskets. Baskets with one variety will make a large mass of color; baskets with mixed varieties can also be very appealing. The second type of basket display is the decorative basket, with dahlias predominating but also including other fresh flowers and filler. Decorative baskets are viewed and judged from front and back.

adorned with a beautiful standing arrangement of dahlias—an example of a creative class for a large show.

Bouquets are always a very popular section in dahlia shows. A suggested scorecard is listed here.

BOUQUET SCORECARD	
Design	20
Color harmony	30
Distinction and creativity	20
Technical aspects and condition	30

Bouquets should be viewed from all sides. The bouquet classes are exhibited using either one variety of dahlia or mixed varieties of dahlias. Mixed bouquets with dahlias predominating but including other flowers are a variation seen at shows.

Baskets of dahlias make large colorful exhibits in dahlia shows, but they can take more blooms than some growers have space to raise. People with smaller plots can grow border plants such as peonies or mignon singles, which take less space and yet whose blooms work well for baskets.

Mixed bouquets with dahlias predominant. Photos by McClaren.

Baskets of one variety. Photos by S. McClaren.

Bowl with single flower without foliage. Photo by McClaren.

Bowl with single flower with unattached foliage. Photo by McClaren.

Basket of one variety. Photo by Alan Fisher.

Dahlias have been displayed in bowls for many years in the home but less frequently in shows. Many societies have a section for dahlias displayed in bowls—a popular display for those who have few flowers to enter. The container plays an important part in enhancing the dahlia bloom. The flowers can be singles, without foliage or with unattached foliage; more than one dahlia of the same color can be used with unattached foliage. A sample scorecard follows:

BOWL SCORECARD	
Technical aspects and condition	40
Distinction and creativity	20
Staging	20
Suitability of container	10
Proportion of bloom to container	10

Potted dahlias are ideal for patios and decks. They are also suitable for apartment dwellers who do not have planting space for dahlias. Shows often have sections for all sizes of potted dahlias. Another sample scorecard:

POTTED DAHLIA SCORECARD	
Cultural perfection	35
Floriferousness	30
Foliage	15
Proportion of plant to container	10
Suitability of container	10

Potted dahlias. Photo by S. McClaren.

Some shows have sections for corsages. They can be single or multiple blooms. The following is a sample scorecard for corsages:

CORSAGE SCORECARD	
Design	30
Distinction	30
Technique	30
Condition	10

Corsage. Photo by S. McClaren.

Since the earliest flower and garden shows in the United States, arrangements have been popular. Arrangements were also one of the earliest special sections in dahlia shows. The show schedule should be followed carefully when entering the arrangement section, for arrangements can vary from very simple to complex. The following is a suggested scorecard for arrangements:

ARRANGEMENT SCORECARD	
Design	40
Color harmony	20
Condition	20
Distinction	10
Expression	10

An arrangement using dahlias. Photo by Alan Fisher.

An entry in the arrangement section of a show. Photo by S. McClaren.

The dried dahlia is a new section for dahlia shows. Several articles in recent dahlia literature have furnished instructions for drying and using dried dahlias. Shows have sections for single dried flowers, triple dried flowers, and displays using dried flowers. Sections of dried flowers are attractive additions to shows. The following is a sample scorecard for dried dahlias:

DRIED DAHLIAS SCORECARD

Color and natural appearance	40
Technique of drying	20
Condition	10
Creativity and design	30

Single dried dahlias. Photo by Alan Fisher.

Photography at dahlia shows is a rapidly growing section. A number of areas are being explored, such as black-and-white photos, color photos, digital photos, and matted and unmatted prints. The following is a sample scorecard for photography:

PHOTOGRAPHY SCORECARD

Quality of bloom(s)	20
Three-dimensional effect	20
Composition	20
Use of light	20
Focus of the subject	10
Staging	10

Each ADS-sanctioned dahlia show must have a standard seedling bench class for scoring new dahlia seedlings. The ADS has specific rules for judging seedlings; any seedling scoring 85 points or above becomes a recognized dahlia and must be introduced by having stock available for the public. The hybridizer carefully selects seedlings that will be shown on the seedling bench. The seedling scoring the highest over 85 in each show receives an ADS achievement award.

Before deciding to exhibit your flowers in a dahlia society show, join a dahlia society; members are always eager to encourage and assist new exhibitors. Seek advice from someone with show experience. Finally, secure a show schedule from the society organizing the show and visit the exhibition hall to familiarize yourself with the facilities. I hope these tips will help clear up the many uncertainties and mysteries facing the first-time exhibitor.

TRIAL GARDENS

Trial gardens have been founded throughout the world for the express purpose of evaluating seedlings. Although there are many similarities from region to region, each country establishes its own set of rules and regulations for entering seedlings. The ADS has established trial gardens in both Canada and the United States so that new seedlings can be evaluated in many climates, soils, and weather conditions, and judged by unbiased judges. Trial gardens are a better test of the health and floriferousness of the dahlia than the seedling bench. A seedling must score 85 or above from either one trial garden or one seedling bench or win two blue ribbons during a show season before it is listed in the *ADS Classification and Handbook of Dahlias*.

The ADS requires that the dahlia is undisseminated, at least four years old, and named before being entered in a trial garden. The hybridizer needs adequate stock available before the variety can be introduced. At the end of the growing season the director of the trial garden provides a report on each seedling to the hybridizer. Complete information from the trial gardens in the United States and Canada is published yearly in the *Bulletin of the American Dahlia Society*.

DAHLIA AWARDS

Various dahlia awards are bestowed annually by the ADS. The Stanley Johnson Award is given each year to the dahlia receiving the greatest number of blue ribbons and higher awards in the previous year; a named variety can receive this award only once.

The Lynn B. Dudley Award is given each year to a new fully double seedling that has the highest average of three scores of 85 or more on the seedling bench.

The Evie Gullikson Award is given each year to a new open-centered seedling that has the highest average of three scores of 85 or more on the seedling bench; it is also awarded annually to a new open-centered seedling that has the highest average of three scores of 85 or more in the trial gardens.

The Derrill W. Hart Award is given each year to a new fully double seedling that has the highest average of three scores of 85 or more in the trial gardens.

Each year since 1974 the ADS lists the Cream of the Crop, dahlias that score the highest in each class or attain a certain number of blue ribbons in combined ADS shows (the Eastern and Mid-Western Dahlia Societies of the United States originated the Cream of the Crop list).

The Fabulous Fifty, initiated by the ADS in 1985, lists all dahlias that receive 50 or more blue ribbons and higher awards each year in combined ADS shows.

Many outstanding dahlias have been show flowers for years. Others score well for a time but soon disappear from the show table; often these flowers have excellent blooms but have weaknesses in the plant or tubers. If the plant is susceptible to virus or other diseases, or has poor tuber production or tubers that don't keep well in storage, the variety will eventually disappear. Several flowers have been consistent winners in ADS shows; a review of past bulletins of the ADS, Cream of the Crop, and Fabulous Fifty yields the following list of the top-three dahlias in their class:

AA	'Bonaventure', 'Inland Dynasty', 'Zorro'
A	'Kidd's Climax', 'Spartacus', 'Hamari Katrina'
B	'Edna C', 'Hamari Accord', 'April Dawn'
BB	'Hamilton Lillian', 'Camano Cloud', 'Taratahi Lilac'
miniature	'Mary Jo', 'Rose Toscano', 'Glenbank Twinkle'
ball	'Brookside Snowball', 'Jessie G', 'Cornel'
miniature ball	'Downham Royal', 'Nettie', 'Barbarry Gem'
pompon	'Poppet', 'Glenplace', 'Yellow Baby'
waterlily	'Red Velvet', 'Nepos', 'Taratahi Ruby'
peony	'Powder Gull', 'Bishop of Llandaff', 'Japanese Bishop'
single	'Alta Bishop', 'Alpen Sparkle', 'First Love'
mignon single	'Rembrandt', 'Matthew Juul', 'Bonne Esperance'
collarette	'Alpen Cherub', 'Christmas Star', 'Elizabeth Snowden'
anemone	'Goldie Gull', 'Azuma Kagami', 'Alpen Fury'
orchid	'Marie Schnugg', 'Honka', 'Amy's Star'
novelty	'Alloway Candy', 'Akita No Hikari', 'Camano Pet'

The highest-scoring dahlia winning the greatest number of awards is 'Edna C', followed closely by 'Hamari Accord'. Varieties winning awards since 2002 are not included in this list.

CHAPTER 13

Dahlia Classification Guide

OVER THE PAST 85 YEARS the American Dahlia Society has developed a system for classifying dahlias. As new dahlias have been hybridized, the Classification Committee of the ADS has continued to update information on form, size, and color. To assist dahlia growers in their understanding, the present ADS classification system, used throughout this book, is presented here.

The *ADS Classification and Handbook of Dahlias* is published annually. Nearly 2000 varieties are listed in alphabetical order and by the assigned ADS class number. In addition, a composite list of all previous versions of the *ADS Classification and Handbook of Dahlias* is periodically updated and published.

The ADS classification system identifies 19 different forms of dahlias with nine of the forms classified by size and all classified by 15 colors. From the combinations of these characteristics the ADS currently recognizes 570 classes. Each class is assigned a three-digit number, which is placed in front of the dahlia name.

Prior to 1975 the ADS identified dahlias only by their name, form, and color; in 1975 the present system, using the three-digit ADS class number, was adopted.

The following information is taken from the *ADS Classification and Handbook of Dahlias*. A special thanks to the Executive Board of the American Dahlia Society and all past and present members of the Classification Committee who have made this possible.

CLASSIFICATION BY SIZE

Nine forms are classified by size; the remaining ten have no size requirements.
The diameter between the outer tips of the mature marginal rays determines the size of the flower.

AA dahlia. Photo by McClaren.

A dahlia. Photo by McClaren.

B dahlia. Photo by McClaren.

BB dahlia. Photo by McClaren.

Miniature dahlia. Photo by McClaren.

Ball dahlia. Photo by S. McClaren.

Miniature ball dahlia. Photo by McClaren.

Pompon dahlia. Photo by McClaren.

Mignon single dahlia. Photo by McClaren.

AA (giant) . . . . over 10 in. (25 cm) in diameter

A (large) . . . . 8 to 10 in. (20 to 25 cm) in diameter

B (medium) . . . . 6 to 8 in. (15 to 20 cm) in diameter

BB (small) . . . . 4 to 6 in. (10 to 15 cm) in diameter

M (miniature) . . . . under 4 in. (10 cm) in diameter

BA (ball) . . . . over 3.5 in. (8.75 cm) in diameter

MB (miniature ball) . . . . 2 to 3.5 in. (5 to 8.75 cm) in diameter

P (pompon) . . . . under 2 in. (5 cm) in diameter

MS (mignon single) . . . . under 2 in. (5 cm) in diameter

CLASSIFICATION BY FORM

For the purpose of classification, each form is assigned fifteen numbers. The following numbers and descriptions identify each form (notice that the straight cactus and incurved cactus are assigned the same fifteen numbers).

The formal decorative, informal decorative, semi-cactus, straight cactus, incurved cactus, laciniated, ball, miniature ball, pompon, waterlily, stellar, and novelty fully double forms are all completely double with the central rays spirally displayed. The mature petal formations that determine the size of the dahlia also determine the dahlia form.

The peony, anemone, collarette, single, mignon single, orchid, and novelty open forms have the disc displayed.

01–15: formal decorative. Ray florets are generally flat, broad, and smooth in a regular arrangement, gradually recurving toward the stem. Each ray floret row should convey uniform and regular size arrangement with the tips preferably round or extending to a slight point. The depth is ideally ¾ the diameter of the bloom and should not be greater than its diameter.

Formal decorative dahlia.
Photo by McClaren.

Shapes of formal decorative ray florets.
Photo by McClaren.

21–35: informal decorative. Ray florets are twisted, curled, or wavy, and have uniform size in irregular arrangement. They may be partially involute or revolute, but no portion should be fully revolute or involute except at the tip of the ray floret. The depth is ideally ¾ the diameter of the bloom and should not be greater than its diameter.

Informal decorative dahlia.
Photo by S. McClaren.

41–55: semi-cactus. Ray florets are broad at base, straight or incurved, and reflex toward the stem in a regular and uniform arrangement. Ray florets will be revolute for approximately ½ their length and fully revolute (touching or overlapping) for at least ¼ their length. The depth is ideally ¾ the diameter of the bloom and should not be greater than its diameter.

Semi-cactus dahlia. Photo by S. McClaren.

61–75: straight cactus. Ray florets are narrow at the base, straight, uniform in length and reflex toward the stem, radiating uniformly in all directions from the center. They will be revolute for the majority of their length and fully revolute (touching or overlapping) for approximately ½ their length. A depth of about ¾ the diameter is ideal for the form.

Straight cactus dahlia. Photo by McClaren.

Incurved cactus dahlia. Photo by Alan Fisher.

61–75: incurved cactus. Ray florets are pointed, uniform in length; they uniformly curve toward the face of the bloom, revolute for the majority of their length and fully revolute for at least ½ their length. Because ray florets curve toward the face of the bloom, they usually lack the depth of the preceding dahlia forms. A depth of ½ the diameter or slightly more is ideal for this form. Although the general direction of the ray floret is up and away from the stem, there may be an arc to the rays, downward and then up. The involucre is rarely if ever covered.

Faces of ray florets (l to r): formal decorative, informal decorative, semi-cactus, cactus, and laciniated. Photo by McClaren.

Reverses of ray florets (l to r): formal decorative, informal decorative, semi-cactus, cactus, and laciniated. Photo by McClaren.

81–95: laciniated. Ray florets are split at the tip with the number and depth of the split varying according to the size of the ray floret. The portion of the ray floret with the splits should uniformly twist or curl whether involute or revolute. The less mature ray florets should possess splits but do not have to twist or curl. In the ideal laciniated dahlia, the majority of ray florets will be uniformly arranged with a split, twist, or curl that conveys an overall fringed or frilled effect. Ray florets, slightly involute or revolute, that split regardless of length and remain generally flat are a major fault. Ray florets with a shallow notch or cleft and possessing little twisting to the extreme portion should not be classified as laciniated. The depth is ideally ¾ the diameter of the bloom and should not be greater than its diameter.

Laciniated dahlia. Photo by S. McClaren.

Ray florets of laciniated dahlia. Photo by McClaren.

501–515: ball. Blooms are ball-shaped with uniform florets, involute for most of their length, and fully involute for more than ½ the length; the ray florets reflex toward the stem. Ray floret tips in cross section should be circular and exhibit little distortion, completely filling the floral head, and are either round or blunt.

Ball dahlia. Photo by S. McClaren.

521–535: miniature ball. Except for size, miniature ball and ball dahlias possess the same form.

Miniature ball dahlia.
Photo by McClaren.

541–555: pompon. The ray florets are involute for the whole of their length and fully involute for ½ their length. Otherwise, apart from size, they are similar to the ball form.

Pompon dahlia. Photo by McClaren.

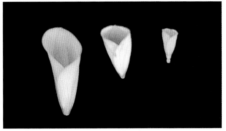

Ray florets (l to r): ball, miniature ball, pompon. Photo by McClaren.

561–575: stellar. Ray florets break gradually from immature florets to fully developed outer ray florets. The outer florets should be narrow and involute with a slight recurve to the stem. The less mature florets should possess the same narrow and partially involute characteristics. The depth of the stellar form should be from ½ to ⅔ the diameter of the bloom, the greater depth being the ideal.

Stellar dahlia. Photo by McClaren.

Ray florets (l to r): pompon (involute), semi-cactus (revolute), incurved cactus (revolute and incurved), and formal decorative (flat). Photo by McClaren.

601–615: waterlily. The bloom should be fully double and symmetrical; the side view should be flat to saucer-shaped in arrangement, and the layer of florets should be open-faced to give a delicate appearance. The center should be closed and dome-shaped, breaking gradually to four to seven fully developed outer florets. Outer florets should be broad and slightly cupped with rounded tips. A bloom position of 45° is preferred, but a top-facing bloom is acceptable. In petite waterlily cultivars, 1 to 3 in. (2.5 to 7.5 cm) in diameter, the depth should contain fewer rows of ray florets in order to represent the waterlily form accurately. The depth should never be more than ½ the diameter of the bloom.

Waterlily dahlia. Photo by S. McClaren.

621–635: peony. Two or more rows of ray florets surround the disc flowers. Ray florets adjacent to the disc flowers may be smaller, twisted, and/or curled.

Peony dahlia. Photo by McClaren.

641–655: anemone. One or more rows of ray florets surround a center of elongated tubular disc flowers. The outer ray florets should be equal in shape, size, and formation, generally flat with rounded tips, and regularly arranged around the disc flowers. Greater visibility of the ray florets from the face is preferred. The tubular disc flowers should be fully developed and present a domed pincushion appearance.

Anemone dahlia. Photo by McClaren.

661–675: collarette. A bloom will have a single row of flat or slightly cupped ray florets arranged in a flat plane; the ray florets will uniformly overlap, preferably in the same direction, with no gaps. The petaloids surrounding the disc should be approximately ½ to ⅔ the length of the ray florets. Eight ray florets is most desirable. A round floret tip is preferred.

Collarette dahlia. Photo by McClaren.

701–715: single. The bloom has a single row of flat or slightly cupped ray florets arranged in a flat plane. They uniformly overlap, preferably in the same direction, with no gaps. Eight ray florets is most desirable. A round floret tip is preferred. The bloom is 2 in. (5 cm) or over in diameter.

Single dahlia. Photo by McClaren.

721–735: mignon single. Mignon single dahlias possess the same form as single dahlias except they must have round floret tips and the bloom is less than 2 in. (5 cm) in diameter.

761–775: novelty open. Dahlias with characteristics distinct and different from the present classifications are classified as novelty dahlias. The center of the novelty open should be open with the disc center in proper proportion to the ray florets.

781–795: novelty fully double. Dahlias with characteristics distinct and different from the present classifications are classified as novelty dahlias. The center of the novelty fully double should be closed.

Mignon single dahlia.
Photo by S. McClaren.

Novelty open dahlia.
Photo by S. McClaren.

Novelty fully double dahlia.
Photo by S. McClaren.

741–755: orchid. A single row of uniform, evenly spaced ray florets arranged in a flat plane surround the disc flowers. The ray florets should be straight and involute for ⅔ or more of their length and fully involute for at least ⅓ their length. Eight ray florets is most desirable.

Orchid dahlia. Photo by McClaren.

CLASSIFICATION BY COLOR

Color classification of a flower is determined by the predominant color or colors appearing on the face of the ray florets except for orchids, which are classified by the color on the reverse of the ray florets. The color of open-centered dahlias is determined by the predominant color(s) of the ray floret, which is listed in capital letter(s) with the predominant color listed first. The colors of the bicolor ray floret tips, petaloids, domes, and eye-zones, where apparent, are listed next in lower-case letters. The official color guide for the ADS is the Royal Horticultural Colour Chart.

For the purpose of classification, all colors, shades, tints, tones, and combinations thereof known to be found in cultivated forms of dahlias have been grouped and subdivided by general color, as follows. The last two numbers of the three-digit ADS class number represent the color of the dahlia. Note that if a bloom in the red class has the least hint of blue in it, it is classified as purple.

W	white
Y	yellow
OR	orange
PK	pink
DP	dark pink
R	red
DR	dark red
L	lavender
PR	purple
LB	light blend
BR	bronze
FL	flame blend
DB	dark blend
V	variegated
BI	bicolor

White dahlia. Photo by Alan Fisher.

Yellow dahlia. Photo by S. McClaren.

Orange dahlia. Photo by S. McClaren.

Pink dahlia. Photo by McClaren.

Dark pink dahlia. Photo by S. McClaren.

Red dahlia. Photo by McClaren.

Dark red dahlia. Photo by McClaren.

Lavender dahlia. Photo by McClaren.

Purple dahlia. Photo by McClaren.

Light blend dahlia. Photo by McClaren.

Bronze dahlia. Photo by McClaren.

Flame blend dahlia. Photo by McClaren.

Dark blend dahlia. Photo by McClaren.

Variegated dahlia. Photo by McClaren.

Bicolor dahlia. Photo by McClaren.

KEY TO CLASS NUMBERS

The following chart is the key to the last two digits of the class number, the digits signifying color, for all nineteen forms: FD (formal decorative), ID (informal decorative), SC (semi-cactus), C (straight cactus), IC (incurved cactus), LC (laciniated), BA (ball), MB (miniature ball), P (pompon), ST (stellar), CO (collarette), WL (waterlily), PE (peony), AN (anemone), S (single), MS (mignon single), O (orchid), NO (novelty open), and NX (novelty fully double).

	FD BA WL S	ID MB PE MS	SC P AN O	C IC CO ST NO	LC NX
Color					
W	01	21	41	61	81
Y	02	22	42	62	82
OR	03	23	43	63	83
PK	04	24	44	64	84
DP	05	25	45	65	85
R	06	26	46	66	86
DR	07	27	47	67	87
L	08	28	48	68	88
PR	09	29	49	69	89
LB	10	30	50	70	90
BR	11	31	51	71	91
FL	12	32	52	72	92
DB	13	33	53	73	93
V	14	34	54	74	94
BI	15	35	55	75	95

The first number of the three-digit ADS class number signifies either size (AA, A, B, BB, M) or form, as follows:

AA	0
A	1
B	2
BB	3
M	4
BA	5
MB	5
P	5
ST	5
WL	6
PE	6
AN	6
CO	6
S	7
MS	7
O	7
NO	7
NX	7

The hybridizer names the dahlia, which can then be classified with its ADS number. For example, let's use these two charts together to find the ADS number of a variegated miniature formal decorative (M FD V): the M is 4, the FD V is 14, and the three digits together form the ADS class number 414. The ADS class number of a pink peony is 624: the first number, for peony, is 6, and a peony that is pink bears the color number of 24. In 127 'Spartacus', the 1 indicates that it is A size, the 27 indicates that it is an informal decorative dark red; for 712 'Parkland Fire', the 7 tells us it's a single and the 12 that it is a flame blend (in ADS shorthand, these dahlias will be classified as 127 Spartacus A ID DR and 712 Parkland Fire S FL, respectively).

The three-digit ADS number classifies all dahlias, indicating the size, form, and color of the dahlia. By using the official ADS Key to Class Numbers from the *ADS Classification and Handbook of Dahlias*, all varieties of dahlias can be classified by ADS number as well as by name.

ADS class number 414 Miniature Formal Decorative Variegated. Photo by McClaren.

ADS class number 712 'Parkland Fire' (S FL). Photo by McClaren.

ADS class number 127 'Spartacus' (A ID DR). Photo by McClaren.

ADS class number 624 Peony Pink. Photo by McClaren.

Resources

One way to become familiar with the dahlia is to join a dahlia society. Many countries have a national society as well as local societies, and many, at both levels, can be found on the Internet. National societies provide valuable information on dahlias, including bulletins, classification handbooks, and judging manuals.

Dahlia growers are always on the lookout for valuable dahlia information. Each year the Puget Sound Dahlia Association publishes *Dahlias of Today*. This outstanding publication can be ordered from Jean Knutson, 7335 34th Ave. SW, Seattle, WA 98126 USA, for $5.00 plus $2.00 shipping.

AMERICAN DAHLIA SOCIETY

Members of the ADS receive the *Bulletin of the American Dahlia Society* quarterly and the *ADS Classification and Handbook of Dahlias* annually. In addition a *Guide to Judging Dahlias* and *A Guide to Growing and Caring for Dahlias* are available for a minimal fee.

American Dahlia Society
President, Ronald Miner
8431 Tulip Ln.
Chagrin Falls, OH 44023 USA
e-mail: baronminer@aol.com
Web site: www.dahlia.org/

ADS Membership
Alan A. Fisher
1 Rock Falls Ct.
Rockville, MD 20854 USA
e-mail: afisherADS@yahoo.com

ADS Bulletin Editor
Norman Hines
364 South 600 West
Hebron, IN 46341 USA

INTERNATIONAL DAHLIA SOCIETIES

Australia

Dahlia Society of New South Wales and Australian Capital Territory
Web site: www.lisp.com.au/~dahlia/

Dahlia Society of South Australia, Inc.
Web site:
www.micronet.net.au/~dahliasa/

National Dahlia Society of Tasmania
Web site:
www.dahlia.org/Australia/tasmania.html

National Dahlia Society of Victoria
10 Murphy Rd.
Doncaster 3108
Victoria
e-mail: pincush@alphalink.com.au
Web site: www.dahlia.org/Australia/AustraliaNDS.html

Queensland Dahlia Society, Inc.
34 Hornby St.
Everton Park 4053
Queensland
Web site: www.dahlia.org/Australia/Queensland.html

Denmark

Danish Dahlia Society
Vangeledet 41
3400 Hillerod
e-mail: Karin.krautwald@intervet.com
Web site: www.dahlia.org/Danish.html

France

Dahlia France
e-mail: dahliaframe@free.fr
Web site: http://dahliafrance.free.fr/

Germany

German Dahlias-,
Fuchsien and Gladiolen Society
Business Guide, Bettina Verbeek
Maasstrasse 153
47608 funds Walbeck
e-mail:
DDFGGinfoverbeek@t_online.de
Web site: www.ddfgg.de/start.htm

India

Dahlia Society of India
12 Bhattacharrjee Para Rd., Plot 5
Calcutta 700063

New Zealand

National Dahlia Society of
New Zealand, Inc.
78 Cameron Rd.
Te Puke, Bay of Plenty
e-mail: Kotaredahlia@xtra.co.nz
Web site: www.dahlia.org/NZ.html

South Africa

South Africa Dahlia Society
48 Caledon St.
Bellville South 7530
e-mail: jandrea@uwc.ac.za
Web site:
www.dahlia.org/SouthAfrica.html

United Kingdom

National Dahlia Society
48 Vickers Rd.
Ash Vale, Aldershot
Hants GU12 5SE
tel: 01252 693003
Web site:
www.dahlia-nds.co.uk/web3.htm

INTERNET RESOURCES

Dahlia-Alert, Dahlia News for Dahlia Growers, is an announcement list and an information source for gardeners with an interest in growing and enjoying spectacular dahlias. It is relatively low in volume and very focused on providing dahlia information you can use at the time you need it. The dahlia-alert service includes e-mailed variety lists, announcements of updates to online supplier sites, and other announcements of general interest to dahlia growers.
Web site: www.groups.yahoo.com/group/dahlia-alert/

Dahlia Locator, The Big List, lists over 7000 variety-to-supplier line items: dahlias arranged alphabetically followed by each commercial grower who might carry the variety. Updated annually.
Website: http://dahlias.net/dbiglist.txt

Dahlia-Net is a place where dahlia growers and those who appreciate dahlias come together to discuss their favorite flower.

You are invited to join in on open discussions and learn about the ADS and dahlia shows.
Web site:
www.groups.yahoo.com/group/dahlia-net/

COMMERCIAL DAHLIA GARDENS: UNITED STATES AND CANADA

Alpen Gardens
29477 SW Ladd Hill Rd.
Sherwood, OR 97140
e-mail: info@alpengardens.com
Web site: www.alpengardens.com

Arlene's Legacy
P.O. Box 5191
Everett, WA 98206-5191
e-mail: Dahlialdy@aol.com
Web site: www.cruger.com/czdahlia.html

Arrowhead Dahlias
10567 Rd. 37
Ft. Lupton, CO 80621
e-mail: ADahlia4U@aol.com
Web site:
www.dahlias.net/htmbox/arrowhead.htm

Art's Nursery Ltd.
8940 192nd St.
Surrey, BC V4N 3W8
e-mail: info@artsnursery.com
Web site: www.artsnursery.com/shopping/dahlias/list.asp

B & D Dahlias
19857 Marine View Dr. SW
Normandy Park, WA 98166
e-mail: bddahlias@foxinternet.net
Web site: http://www.bddahlias.com/

Bridge View Dahlia Gardens
1876 Maple St.
North Bend, OR 97459
e-mail: madja@worldnet.att.net
Web site:
http://www.cruger.com/bvdahlia.html

Camano Dahlias
2221 Harnden Loop
Camano Island, WA 98292
e-mail: ambrosed@whidbey.net
Web site:
www.dahlias.net/htmbox/camano.htm

Canadahlia Gardens
82 Clifton Downs Rd.
Hamilton, ON L9C 2P3

Capistrano Dahlia Gallery
547 Capistrano Dr.
Kalispell, MT 59901

Carousel Dahlias
P.O. Box 9
Soap Lake, WA 98851
e-mail: toiman@2fast.net
Web site:
www.dahlias.net/htmbox/carousel.htm

Chesterfield Dahlia Farm
68 South Main St.
Cranbury, NJ 08512
e-mail: Info@dahliafarm.com
Web site: www.dahliafarm.com

Chinook Country Glads
21 2nd St. NE
High River, AB T1V 1G6
e-mail: powys@telusplanet.net

CJ's Dahlias
6548 Tracyton Blvd. NW
Bremerton, WA 98311

Clack's Dahlia Patch
5585 N Myrtle Creek Rd.
Myrtle Creek, OR 97457
e-mail: cladp@wizzard.net
Web site: www.cruger.com/cddahlia.html

Clearview Dahlias
20212 65th Ave. SE
Snohomish, WA 98296
e-mail: parshalld@prodigy.net

Connell's
10616 Waller Rd. E
Tacoma, WA 98446
e-mail: connells@oz.cet.com
Web site: www.connells-dahlias.com

Cook Lane Dahlias
31215 Kent-Black Diamond Rd.
Auburn, WA 98092
e-mail: cooklanedahlias@aol.com
Web site: www.dahlias-online.com

Corralitos Gardens
41 Pine Hill Rd.
Corralitos, CA 95076
e-mail: kevinlarkin@msn.com
Web site: www.corralitosgardens.com

Cottontail Gardens
P.O. Box 2971
Mt. Vernon, WA 98273
e-mail: cottontailgarden@aol.com

Creekside Dahlia Farm
3447 Whitepath Rd.
Ellijay, GA 30540
e-mail: killer@ellijay.com

Crown Point Dahlia Gardens
63239 Crown Point Rd.
Coos Bay, OR 97420
Web site: www.geocities.com/
crownptdahliagardens

Dahlia Dandies
1717 S Woodland Dr.
Kalispell, MT 59901
Web site: www.valler.com/dahlia/

Dahlias by Viv & Les Connell
6807 154th Place SE
Snohomish, WA 98296-8600
e-mail: beaucon11@msn.net

Dahlias Galore
5245 Selma Park Rd.
Sechelt, BC V0N 3A2
e-mail: dahlias@dccnet.com
Web site: www.dahliasgalore.com

Dan's Dahlias
994 South Bank Rd.
Oakville, WA 98568
e-mail: sales@dansdahlias.com
Web site: www.dansdahlias.com

Danielle's Dahlias
11342 West Orchard
Nampa, ID 83651
e-mail: info@dahliasplus.com
Web site: www.dahliasplus.com

Dick's Dahlias
11 South Fairfield
Round Lake, IL 60073
e-mail: dicksdahlias@aol.com
Web site: www.geocities.com/
dicksdahlias

Distinctive Dahlias
P.O. Box 453
Valier, MT 59486
e-mail: kendeide@hotmail.com

Dolinski & Son
779 East Avenue
Franklinville, NJ 08080
e-mail: dolinski@snip.net
Web site: http://users.snip.net/~dolinski

E & S Dahlias, Inc.
468 Shaw Rd.
Berwick North, NS B0P 1E0
e-mail: rbbluenoser@ns.sympatico.ca
Web site: www.dahlias.net/htmbox/
esalley.htm

Elkhorn Gardens
P.O. Box 1149
Carmel, CA 93921
e-mail: Dahlias@elkhorngardens.com
Web site: www.elkhorngardens.com

Emerald Valley Farm
88589 Chukar Ln.
Veneta, OR 97487

Farmer Creek Gardens
27850 Hwy 101 S
Cloverdale, OR 97112
e-mail:
FarmerCrkGardens@oregoncoast.com
Web site: http://www.nvo.com/
farmercrkgarden

Ferncliff Gardens
8502 McTaggart St.
Mission, BC V2V 6S6
US mailing: Box 66, Sumas, WA 98295
e-mail: info@ferncliffgardens.com
Web site: www.ferncliffgardens.com

Frey's Dahlias
12054 Brick Rd.
Turner, OR 97332
e-mail: freydahlias@juno.com
Web site: www.freysdahlias.com

Garden Valley Dahlias
406 Lower Garden Valley Rd.
Roseburg, OR 97470
e-mail: gvdahlia@mcsi.net
Web site:
www.cruger.com/gvdahlia.html

Gordon Leroux Dahlias
5021 View Dr.
Everett, WA 98203-2423
e-mail: gorjean@aol.com
Web site: www.dahlias.net/htmbox/
gleroux.htm

GW's Flowers
2397 Boone Ford Rd. SE
Calhoun, GA 30701
e-mail: kingdahlia@att.net
Web site:
www.dahlias.net/htmbox/gwflowers.htm

Hamilton Dahlia Farm
4710 South St.
Hamilton, MI 49419
e-mail: info@dahlia.com
Web site: www.dahlia.com

Heartland Dahlia Garden
804 E Vistula
Bristol, IN 46507
e-mail: dahlia@peoplepc.com
Web site:
www.heartlanddahliagarden.com

Helen's Dahlias
6813 NE 139th St.
Vancouver, WA 98686
e-mail: dhbair@pacifier.com
Web site: http://dahlia-
world.netfirms.com/HD.html

Homestead Gardens
125 Homestead Rd.
Kalispell, MT 59901
e-mail: hggarden@bigsky.net
Web site:
www.dahlias.net/htnbox/homestead.htm

Island Dahlias
1270 Mayfair Rd.
Comox, BC V9M 4C2
e-mail: bush@mars.ark.com.ca
Web site:
www.dahlias.net/htmbox/island.htm

J & C Dahlias
3822 163rd St. E
Tacoma, WA 98446
e-mail: JCDahlias@aol.com
Web site:
http://hometown.aol.com/jcdahlias/
JCDahlias.html

J T Dahlias
P.O. Box 20967
Greenfield, WI 53220
e-mail: jtdahlias@msn.com

Korb Dahlias
636 36th Ave. SE
Albany, OR 97321

La Connor Dahlias
P.O. Box 329
La Conner, WA 98257

Lakewood Dahlia Garden
312 Beach Rd.
Wolcott, CT 06716

Lobaugh's Dahlias
113 Ramsey Rd.
Chehalis, WA 98532
e-mail: contact@lobdahlia.cjb.net
Web site: http://www.lobdahlia.cjb.net/

Lois' Choice Dahlias
22041 Peter Grubb Rd. SE
Renton, WA 98058-0416

Merlin's Dahlia Farm
P.O. Box 485
Port Angeles, WA 98362
e-mail: merlin@olypen.com

Minerva Dahlias
2525 Jordan Rd.
Columbus, OH 43231
e-mail: a11b17@aol.com

Mingus Dahlias
7407 NE 139th St.
Vancouver, WA 98662
e-mail: pjmingus@pacifier.com
Web site:
http://www.dahliasuppliers.com/mingus/

Mohawk Dahlia Garden
P.O. Box 898
Marcola, OR 97454
e-mail: mohawkdahlias@aol.com
Web site:
www.dahlias.net/htmbox/mohawk.htm

Oak Hill Dahlias
978 310th St.
Atalissa, IA 52720
e-mail: oakhillacr@aol.com

Old House Gardens
536 W Third St.
Ann Arbor, MI 48103
e-mail: OHGBulbs@aol.com
Web site: www.oldhousegardens.com/

Parks Dahlias
661 Starveout Creek Rd.
Azalea, OR 97410
e-mail: cparks@internetcds.com
Web site:
www.cruger.com/pkdahlia.html

Pioneer Dahlias
Box 384
Burlington, WA 98233
e-mail: info@pioneerdahlias.com
Web site: www.pioneerdahlias.com

Pleasant Valley Glads & Dahlias
87 Edward St.
P.O. Box 494
Aqawam, MA 01001
e-mail: pleasantvalleyglads@attbi.com
Web site: www.gladiola.com

Reynolds Dahlias
37800 Sodaville Cutoff
Lebanon, OR 97355

Sauvie Island Dahlias
26750 NW Sauvie Island Rd.
Portland, OR 97231
e-mail: IMSEEDY@aol.com
Web site: www.sauvieislanddahlias.com/
sauvie.html

S B Gardens
12027 62nd Ave. S
Seattle, WA 98178
e-mail: sbgseattle@aol.com
Web site:
http://hometown.aol.com/sbgseattle/
index.html

Sea-Tac Gardens
20020 Des Moines Memorial Dr.
Seattle, WA 98198
e-mail: patheck@prodigy.com
Web site:
http://pages.prodigy.net/patheck/
index.html

Showcase Dahlias
3609 NE 91st St.
Vancouver, WA 98665
e-mail: showcasedahlias@yahoo.com

Skipley Dahlias
7508 Skipley Rd.
Snohomish, WA 98290-5132

Suttell's Dahlias
5543 Blezard Dr.
Beamsville, ON L0R 1B3

Swan Island Dahlias
P.O. Box 700
Canby, OR 97013-0700
e-mail: info@dahlias.com
Web site: www.dahlias.com

TLC Dahlias
332 Parliament Dr.
Kalispell, MT 59901
e-mail: tlcdahlia@in-tch.com
Web site:
www.dahlias.net/htmbox/tlcgarden.htm

Valley Flower Farm
P.O. Box 115
Chimacum, WA 98325-0115
e-mail: smithdl@olympus.net

Valley Flower Garden
2828 Zee Ln. NE
Keizer, OR 97303

White Flower Farm
P.O. Box 50
Litchfield, CT 06759
e-mail: custserv@whiteflowerfarm.com
Web site:
https://www.whiteflowerfarm.com/

Windhaven Court of Honor Dahlias
1107 E Windhaven Rd.
Pittsburgh, PA 15205

Wynne's Dahlias
1395 Willey's Lake Rd.
Ferndale, WA 98248
e-mail: wildwoodrose@msn.com
Web site:
www.dahlias.net/htmbox/wynnes.htm

COMMERCIAL DAHLIA GARDENS: INTERNATIONAL

Belle Fleur Gardens
Northope 4RD
Invercargill, Southland
New Zealand
Web site:
www.friars.co.nz/gardens/pages/
bellefleur.html

Country Dahlias
195 Mathison Rd.
Winchelsia 3241
Victoria, Australia
Web site: www.nurseriesonline.com.au/
countrydahlias

Dahlias Combe-Laboissiere
26800 Ambonil
France
e-mail: francois.combe-
laboissiere@wanadoo.fr
Web site: http://dahliafrance.free.fr/
producteurs/ListeCombe.htm

Devon Dahlias
8 Petrel Place
St. Helens 7216
Tasmania, Australia
Web site:
www.cruger.com/dvdahlia.html

Geerlings Dahlias
Kadijk 38
2104 AA Heemstede
Holland
e-mail: info@geerlings-dahlias.nl
Web site: http://www.geerlings-dahlia.nl

German suppliers, links
Web site: http://www.ddfgg.de/
index_bezugsquellen.htm

Halls of Heddon
Heddon on the Wall
Newcastle upon Tyne NEI5 OJS
United Kingdom
e-mail: hallsofheddon@breathemail.net
Web site: www.hallsofheddon.co.uk

JRG Dahlias
22 Summerville Rd.
Milnthorpe, Cumbria LA7 7DF
United Kingdom
e-mail: jack@jrg-dahlias.co.uk
Web site: www.jrg-
dahlias.co.uk/index.htm

Kingsley Dahlias
139 Goollelal Dr.
Kingsley 6026
Western Australia, Australia
e-mail: Kingsley_Dahlias@excite.com
Web site:
http://members.optusnet.com.au/
~kingdah

Lynrex Gardens
Goulburn Valley Hwy
Mangalor 3663
Australia
e-mail: lynrex@mcmedia.com.au

Murielle Hairon
Le Haut du Parc
50580 Fierville les Mines
France
Web site: http://dahliafrance.free.fr/
producteurs/ListeHairon.htm

Oscroft's
Warwick Rd.
Chadwick End Nr. Solihull B93 0BP
United Kingdom
Web site:
www.dahlia-nds.co.uk/osclist.htm

Station House Nurseries
e-mail: comsales@eurodahlia.com
Web site: www.eurodahlia.com/

Verwer Bros Netherlands
Web site: www.verwer-dahlias.nl

Yusaku Konishi
455 Chibadera
Chuo-ku, Chiba Shi
Japan

ORGANIC GARDENING SUPPLIES

The following U.S. concerns offer organic gardening supplies. Additional suppliers throughout the world are listed on the Internet:
http://organicgardensupplies.com

Abundant Life Seed Foundation
P.O. Box 772
Port Townsend, WA 98368
e-mail: abundant@olypen.com
Web site: www.abundantlifeseed.org

Bountiful Gardens
18001 Shafer Ranch Rd.
Willits, CA 95490-9626
e-mail: bountiful@sonic.net
Web site: www.bountifulgardens.org

Gardens Alive
5100 Schenley Pl.
Lawrenceburg, IN 47025
Web site: www.gardensalive.com

J. L. Hudson, Seedman
Star Route 2, Box 337
La Honda, CA 94020
Web site: www.jlhudsonseeds.net

Johnny's Selected Seeds
184 Foss Hill Rd., RR 1 Box 2580
Albion, ME 04910-9731
Web site: www.johnnyseeds.com

Peaceful Valley
P.O. Box 2209
Grass Valley, CA 95945
Web site: www.groworganic.com

Planet Natural
1612 Gold Ave.
Bozeman, MT 59715
Web site: www.planetnatural.com/

Shepherd's Garden Seeds
30 Irene St.
Torrington, CT 06790-6658
Web site: www.shepherdseeds.com

Territorial Seed Company
P.O. Box 158
Cottage Grove, OR 97424-0061
Web site: www.territorialseed.com

SOURCES FOR SPECIES DAHLIAS

Heronswood Nursery
7530 NE 288th St.
Kingston, WA 98346-9502 USA
Web site: www.heronswood.com

Jim and Jenny Archibald
'Bryn Collen', Ffostrasol
Llandysul SA44 5SB
United Kingdom

Seedhunt
P.O. Box 96
Freedom, CA 95019-0096 USA
e-mail: seedhunt@aol.com
Web site: www.seedhunt.com

Terms and Abbreviations

GLOSSARY

anther. The pollen-bearing portion of the stamen.

bicolor. Two distinct clear and sharply separated colors on the face of the ray florets.

blend. Two or more colors that gradually merge but are distinguishable from a distance of 6 ft. (1.8 m).

bract. Reduced or modified leaf often in the inflorescence.

central rays. The short or immature ray florets comprising the central portion of the fully double flowers when at their prime stage.

class. Dahlias with the same form, size, and color.

cultivar. A named, cultivated, hybridized variety of a plant; in dahlia terminology it is interchangeable with **variety**.

decussate. Arranged in pairs, each at right angles to the next pair above or below.

disbranch. Remove the secondary branches at the leaf node to limit the number of blooms.

disbud. Early removal of the two side buds from the terminal bud.

disc. A more or less flat circular group of tubular florets fully visible in open-centered dahlias.

disc florets. Small tubular florets that make up the disc flower, each with a pistil and stamen.

eye-zone. The band of a contrasting color or colors surrounding the disc of the open-centered flower on the ray florets.

floret. The small flowers that collectively comprise the flower head.

floriferous. Bearing many flowers freely.

fully double. Flower heads with multiple rows of ray florets; the disc flowers are immature and completely covered by the central rays when the flower is at the prime stage.

hardening-off. The process of moving plants outdoors by placing them in a shaded protected area to gradually strengthen the plant tissue for transplanting to the garden.

incurved. The ray florets curve forward along their length toward the face of the flower head.

involucre. The collection of bracts that encloses the bud.

involute. Margins of the ray florets roll forward along the longitudinal axis. When fully involute the margins touch or overlap so only the reverse of the florets is visible.

laciniated. The ray florets are split with a twisting in the area of the split, resulting in both involution and revolution of the petal edges, giving an overall fringed effect.

marginal rays. Fully developed mature ray florets that determine the maximum diameter of a flower.

open-centered flower. A flower head with ray florets surrounding the visible disc.

node. A slightly swollen area on the stem where leaves, branches, and axially buds originate.

petal. The common name for the conspicuously colored part of a floret.

petaloids. Additional floral parts on ray florets that have the form and appearance of small petals, most noticeable in the collarette dahlia.

pistil. The seed-bearing organ of the flower comprised of the ovary and stigma.

pollen. The yellow powder produced by the anthers which functions as the male element in fertilization.

ray florets. The single petal of the flower head forming the border in the open-centered dahlias, or, massed together, the flower head in fully double dahlias.

recurved. A ray floret curving along the axis toward the stem.

revolute. Margins of the ray florets roll backward along their length, and, when fully revolute, the margins touch or overlap.

sport. A change in the color, form, size, or other characteristic in the plant or flower caused by a mutation.

stamen. The pollen-bearing portion of the flower structure in the disc made up of the anther and a filament.

stigma. The divided tip of the pistil, which receives the pollen.

straight cactus. The ray florets have little or no curvature throughout their length.

variegated. Two or more distinct colors on the face of the ray florets, the variegating color arranged in sharply delineated dots, flecks, splashes, stripes, or narrow lines, which contrast with the basic color.

variety. See **cultivar**

DAHLIA ABBREVIATIONS

Dahlia forms

AN	anemone
BA	ball
C	straight cactus
CO	collarette
FD	formal decorative
IC	incurved cactus
ID	informal decorative
LC	laciniated
MB	miniature ball
MS	mignon single
NO	novelty open
NX	novelty fully double
O	orchid
P	pompon
PE	peony
S	single
SC	semi-cactus
ST	stellar
WL	waterlily

Dahlia colors

BI	bicolor
BR	bronze
DB	dark blend
DP	dark pink
DR	dark red
FL	flame blend
L	lavender
LB	light blend
OR	orange
PK	pink
PR	purple
R	red
V	variegated
W	white
Y	yellow

Bibliography

Bailey, L. H. 1895. Meetings of Societies. *Garden and Forest* 399 (October): 418–419. Cornell University.

Giannasi, D. E. 1975. Flavonoid Chemistry and Evolution in *Dahlia* (Compositae). *Bulletin of the Torrey Botanical Club* 102:404–412.

Hansen, Hans V., and J. P. Hjerting. 1996. Observations on Chromosome Numbers and Biosystemics on *Dahlia* (Asteraceae, Heliantheae) with an Account on the Identity of *D. pinnata*, *D. rosea*, and *D. coccinea*. *Nordic Journal of Botany* 16 (4).

Lawrence, W. J. C. 1929. The Genetics and Cytology of *Dahlia* Species. *Journal of Genetics* 21:125.

Saar, D. E. 2002. *Dahlia neglecta* (Asteraceae, Coreopsideae), a new species from Sierra Madre Oriental, Mexico. *Sida* 20:593–596.

Saar, D. E., N. O. Polans, and P. D. Sorensen. 2003. A Phylogenetic Analysis of the Genus *Dahlia* (Asteraceae) Based on Internal and External Transcribed Spacer Regions of Nuclear Ribosomal DNA. *Systematic Botany* 28(3): 627–639.

Sherff, E. E., and E. J. Alexander. 1955. *Dahlia*. In *North American Flora*. New York Botanical Garden.

Smith, W. M. 1830. *On Dahlias*. Horticultural Society of London.

Sorensen, P. D. 1969. Revision of the Genus *Dahlia* (Compositae, Heliantheae, Coreopsidinae). *Rhodora* 71:309–416.

Stout, Mrs. Charles H. 1922. *The Amateur's Book of the Dahlia*. Doubleday, Page & Company. Garden City, New York.

Weland, Gerald. 1996. History of the Garden Dahlia. *Bulletin of the American Dahlia Society* (September): 69–79.

———. 1997a. History of the Garden Dahlia. *Bulletin of the American Dahlia Society* (March): 75–87.

———. 1997b. History of the Garden Dahlia. *Bulletin of the American Dahlia Society* (June): 42–60.

Willdenow, K. L. 1810. The Dahlia. *Species plantarum*.

Subject Index

Photo Cultivar Index